LUNAR SURFACE WARFARE 1960

WARGAMING RULES AND SCENARIOS

CHRIS FLAHERTY

SOLDIERSHOP PUBLISHING

AUTHORS

Since 2009, **Chris Flaherty** has written for the UK Armourer Magazine; Classic Arms & Militaria; and Soldier of the Queen Journal. He has advised various art galleries and museums on uniforms. For Partizan Press in 2014, he wrote and illustrated two books: Turkish Uniforms of the Crimean War: A Handbook of Uniforms; and The Ottoman Army in the First World War: A Handbook of Uniforms. He co-authored and illustrated with Bruno Mugnai for Soldiershop Publishing: 2014 Der Lange Turkenkrieg (1593-1606), Volume. 1: The Long Turkish – War Habsburg Arrests the Ottoman Advance; and, in 2015 Der Lange Turkenkrieg (1593-1606), Volume. 2: The Long Turkish War. In 2015, Chris Flaherty was a contributor (illustrator) to the Turkish Gallipoli Centenary Exhibition: From Depths to the Trenches: Gallipoli 1915, at the Isbank Museum in Istanbul.

Chris Flaherty has authored and illustrated for Partizan Press' Universal Wargames Rules Supplements: 'Napoleonic Small Siege, River Ship, Gunboat and Pontooning' (2016); 'Napoleonic Foraging, Insurrection, Marauders, Bakeries, Convoy and Encampment Wargaming' (2016); 'Napoleonic Balloon Warfare' (2017); 'Napoleonic Ottoman Army Wargaming Supplement' (2018); 'A Wargamer's Guide to WW1 Ottoman Army Uniforms' (2018); 'Napoleon's July 1798 Pyramid Campaign & the Egyptian Army' (2019); 'The Napoleonic Ottoman Army: Uniforms, Tactics and Organization' (2019). In 2021 he wrote and illustrated 'The Sardinian Expeditionary Corps' for Soldiershop Publishing.

INDEX

Title: LUNAR SURFACE WARFARE 1960 - Wargaming Rules and Scenarios
By Chris Flaherty
Serie Paper Battles&Dioramas edit by Luca S. Cristini. First edition by Soldiershop series. November 2021
Cover & Art Design: Luca S. Cristini. ISBN code: 978-88-93277952
Published by Luca Cristini Editore, via Orio 35/4- 24050 Zanica (BG) ITALY. www.soldiershop.com

INTRODUCTION

This short book on Lunar Surface Warfare in the 1960s, presents a set of wargaming rules for combat between Soviet Cosmonauts and United States Army and Airforce Soldier-Astronauts. It is based on early popular science, and military studies conducted in the 1950s, and 1960s that looked at how the U.S. Army, or Airforce would establish a military presence on the Earth's Moon, and would defend that against the Soviets. These pre-Apollo Era studies occurred before the creation of the 1967 Outer Space Treaty that to this day broadly bans the stationing of Weapons of Mass Destruction in Outer Space, and prohibits military activities on celestial bodies, including the Earth's Moon[1]. The following short volume returns to the era between 1948 and 1965, where popular science publications, United States Army and Airforce concepts for establishing a Lunar Base, and the type of weaponry and tactics envisaged for the Lunar Surface were articulated. Envisioning new military capabilities that would fundamentally shift post-WW2 global strategy into the First Space Age – anticipating a new strategic reality, "once … [the first Astronaut] … stakes the Earth's satellite for his country."[2] It was believed that this one act, would: "set the scene for world-shattering war, unless Earthmen meanwhile find peaceful means of settling their disputes."[3]

THE STRATEGIC IMPERATIVE FOR A LUNAR BASE

In the mid-1950s, beyond occupation of the Moon, a more radical demonstration of military power, was a plan to detonate a Nuclear weapon on the Lunar Surface, with the aim of achieving:

> "certain military objectives would be served since information would be supplied concerning the environment of Space, concerning detection of Nuclear device testing in Space and concerning the capability of Nuclear weapons for Space Warfare."[45]

The possibilities for an Invasion Base on the Moon was envisaged in an 1948 popular science concept for such a military enclave on the Lunar Surface, stating that a hostile government would see, "the crater floors of the Moon are natural launching platforms for guided missiles."[6] It was called an Invasion Base, reflecting the idea that it would serve as the launch-point in Space, for a reconquest of the Earth, should a defeat there have happened. The 1961 U.S. Airforce Lunex Launch Complex – a concept for a Lunar Base, which envisaged: "[establishing] … a Lunar Base and the complete conquest of this body … [– the Moon]"[7]. This somewhat reflected the later 1940s popular science language, namely: "the first nation to establish a Lunar military outpost will rule the Earth."[8]

1	United Nations.
2	Ley, 1948.
3	Ley, 1948.
4	Reiffel, 1959.
5	Gault, 2013.
6	Ley, 1948.
7	U.S. Airforce, 1961.
8	Ley, 1948.

The notion of a Lunar Strategy: the use of the Earth's Moon, as a place to attack the Earth's Surface or a potential source of military threat to a country on the Earth, was originally conceived in the 1950s, as a Bi-Planetary Strategy[9][10]. Largely a punch, counter-punch set of exchanges, not unlike the two boxers fighting in the dark[11]. Adding the Moon into the mix, effectively created a third boxer in the dark.

Another Space Strategy that had come into existence at the end of WW2, was the ability to Circumnavigate the Earth[12], and this was related to the Orbital Bomber concept. Earth Circumnavigation and the Orbital Bomber was linked to the notion of, "control of high ground"[13]. At the same time in the 1950s, the same high-ground concept was also related to having a Lunar Base:

> "The Moon provides a retaliation base of unequalled advantage. If we had a base on the Moon, either the Soviets must launch an overwhelming Nuclear attack towards the Moon from Russia two to two-and-one-half days prior to attacking the continental U.S. (and such launchings could not escape detection) or Russia could attack the continental U.S. first, only and inevitably to receive, from the Moon – some 48 hours later, sure and massive destruction."[14][15]

The Bi-Planetary Strategy postulated a third boxer in the dark (on the Moon), fighting alongside one of the two principal boxers in a match (the U.S. and Soviets on Earth). This third boxer coming-in from the depth of Space could be the strategic game-changer in a war:

> "[on] … the Moon may plot the attack that will open World War III. For the man in the Moon will be a powerful 'spy in the sky' rocketed to the Earth's satellite by the aggressor nation to prepare the way for an all-out assault to conquer the World. The nation that sent him there will have a Lunar Base that will expose any spot on Earth to celestial spying and sudden rocket invasion. The Moon's terrain, scarred with countless craters, has thousands of excellent sites for offensive bases. The aggressor who sets up the first interplanetary outpost on the Moon can dominate not only the World but the entire Solar System … In a single historic flight he will have eliminated from the vocabulary of the world's nations the term military security."[16]

It was believed focusing high-powered telescopic lenses on the Earth, this would give observing Soldier-Astronauts a complete panoptic view of the Earth's Surface, and complete Intelligence Dominance over potential enemy countries[17][18].

---

9   Boushey, 1958.
10   Sambaluk, 2011.
11   Hart, 1920.
12   Clarke, 1945
13   Sambaluk, 2011.
14   Boushey, 1958.
15   Sambaluk, 2011.
16   Ley, 1948.
17   Ley, 1948.
18   Borch, 2021.

There were other reasons as well, expressed for the existence of a Lunar Base, in terms of the U.S. Army getting ahead of the Soviets in the Space Race, namely:

> "a Lunar outpost … is of critical importance to the U.S. Army of the future. It was March 1959, and Lieutenant General Arthur G. Trudeau, the writer of those words, was tasking Major General John H. Hinrichs, the Army's Chief of Ordnance, to develop a proposal for a manned Lunar outpost that would protect potential United States interests on the Moon."[19]

It was thought that, "[once] … Moon-Based weapons were in place, it could protect U.S. interests both on Earth and on the Moon." [20] The military proponents argued in the late 1950s that the ultimate strategic goal on the Moon should be to deploy Moon-Based weapons systems. This would serve as a strong deterrent to war, since an enemy would have great difficulty in preventing a U.S. retaliation. It was believed, rivals such as the Soviet Union, or China in that period, would have faced considerable technological challenges reaching the Moon. Whereas, if U.S. military forces were already present on the Moon, they could counter or neutralize any hostile force that might try to land. Effectively, a military race to the Moon. It was considered the first force to reach the Moon and establish a military outpost there, could counter any enemy attempt to land on the Moon thereafter.

UNDERGROUND LUNAR BASES

The 1948 popular science conception of a Lunar Base was use of a Moon crater, taking advantage of the high circular rim used as a bunker against external bomb blasts[21]. The upthrust of the lava rock identified as a common centre feature, in some of the large Lunar craters (as far as these could be made-out from Earth in the late 1940s by telescope) was seen as a possible elevated platform for a Control Dome. Around the Control Dome, it was proposed a ring of concrete launching pits with connecting service roads would be built within the crater. Lunar Bases were envisaged underground - occupying a large, and deep cave shelter engineered with an airlock. It was further noted:

> "If the Moon men find no natural cave, they can make an artificial one by tunnelling about 500 feet into a mountain."[22]

Underground places, either naturally occurring, or tunnelled, could be converted into pressurized structures housing Humans. A buried Lunar Base gave rise to the thinking it would be protected from an attack, or a meteor strike. The strategy was advised by the 1959 U.S. Army Project Horizon Report[23][24]; and, by the 1961 U.S. Airforce Lunex Launch Complex[25]. The basic proposal

---

19   Borch, 2021.
20   Borch, 2021.
21   Ley, 1948.
22   Ley, 1948.
23   U.S. Army, 1959.
24   Borch, 2021.
25   U.S. Airforce, 1961.

was for a deep buried cylindrical structure made from a set of large pipe segments joined end-to-end, with an airlock to the surface. The segments included living quarters, dining and recreation rooms, laboratory and hospital facilities. Having underground structures also solved the extreme surface temperature changes brought about by the month-long Lunar Cycle of two-weeks days and nights; that can have temperature extremes estimated to range between 248 degrees Fahrenheit: 120 degrees Celsius (Lunar day) and minus 202 degrees Fahrenheit: minus 130 degrees Celsius (Lunar night).

CIRCUMLUNAR ORBITAL MILITARY FACILITY

The 1961 U.S. Airforce Lunex Launch Complex, in addition to a Lunar Base also envisaged: "military facilities may have been established … in orbit around the Moon."[26] The notion of a Circumlunar Orbital Military Facility was also found in the 1959 U.S. Army Project Horizon Report, which had an Intermediate Orbiting Space Station[27][28]. Used initially to establish a Lunar Base, it was used as a Space assembly point orbiting the Moon. From this, a Space Transport Vehicle was envisage being used to ferry payloads to the Lunar Surface. The 1959 U.S. Army Project Horizon Report proposal had a plan for 252 men in Earth Orbit by the end of 1967[29]. It was planned that a detail – estimated to be some 42 Soldier-Astronauts would continue onto the Moon for their tours of duty. Some 26 Soldier-Astronauts would then return from the Moon (leaving the Task Force of up to 12 to do their tour at the Lunar Base). The stopping-off point would be the Intermediate Orbiting Space Station before returning home to Earth. The U.S. Army planned for the men to do a tour of duty on the Moon not exceeding one year. In terms of force options, this arrangement appears to have created two reserve forces: (1) A large force: some 200 Soldier-Astronauts on the Earth Orbiting Space Station (some two-three days flight from the Moon); and, (2) a second force of 12 or more Soldier-Astronauts on the Intermediate Orbiting Space Station (awaiting their return-flight to Earth). This arrangement would have given three potential U.S. Army forces of Soldier-Astronauts, who could be directed towards Lunar military operations, if the situation there was to have escalated for any reason, such as fending-off an attack:

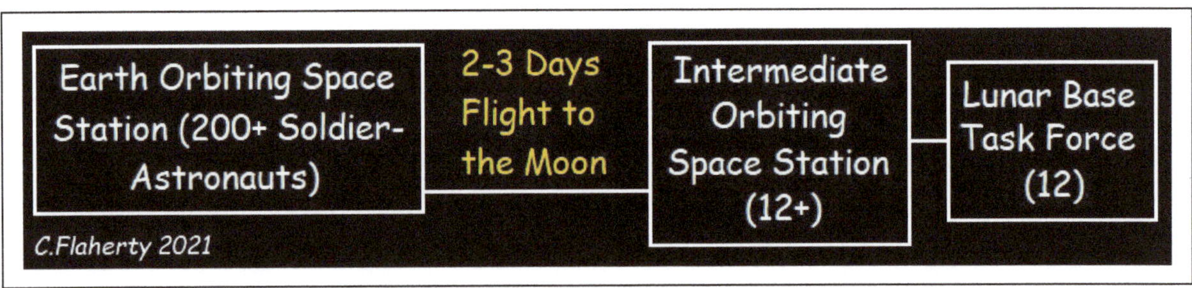

---

26   U.S. Airforce, 1961.

27   U.S. Army, 1959.

28   Borch, 2021.

29   Borch, 2021.

LUNAR SURFACE COMBAT

Potential for some type of military threat to a Lunar Base was raised by the 1959 U.S. Army Project Horizon Report proposal:

> "Initially the outpost will be of sufficient size and contain sufficient equipment to permit the survival and moderate constructive activity of a minimum number of personnel (about 10-20) on a sustained basis. It must be designed for expansion of facilities, resupply, and rotation of personnel to insure maximum extension of sustained occupancy. It should be designed to be self-sufficient for as long as possible without outside support. In the location and design of the base, consideration will be given to operation of a triangulation station of a Moon-to-Earth Base Line Space Surveillance System, facilitating communications with and observation of the Earth, facilitating travel between the Moon and the Earth, exploration of the Moon and further explorations of Space, and to the defence of the base against attack if required."[30]

As to the last requirement - the defence of the base against attack if required, the 1965 U.S. Army Lunar Surface Weapons Study gave greater definition to the notion of Lunar Surface Combat, and how this might be conducted using actual Soldier-Astronauts[31]. These early papers enunciated key tactical concepts that remain relevant to this day in the realm of Space and Lunar Surface Combat Operations. The most significant of which was a radical redefinition of the enduring features of terrestrial tactics, as these were traditionally understood on Earth, than what was expected to operate on the Lunar Surface. This led to a new concept of lethality: penetration and lethality on the Moon are almost synonymous. Meaning that any rip in a Spacesuit, or puncture of a pressurized Human habitat could be immediately catastrophic. Correspondingly the resulting mass of a projectile did not need to be that great.

Under Lunar tactical constraints any type of force concentration would likely prove catastrophic. The destructive power of weapons on the Lunar Surface, or in Space led to only a small force envisaged for a Lunar Base, namely: "a final complement of 12 men"[32]. Significantly, Soviet planners also came to a similar conclusion in regards to their own Lunar Base concept – the Zvezda Moon Base-Train, was designed for roughly the same number of Cosmonauts. Perhaps a slightly larger civilian component would also have been at a Lunar Base, for scientific, exploration or construction purposes. Given the low numbers envisaged, neither side: Soviet or United States in a conflict would have a great deal of forces to spare.

The concept of distance, weapons effect and range, and the use of terrain were all envisaged to radically change, than were typically seen on Earth. New weapons were envisaged, designed to fit new parameters based on the Moon's surface conditions and harsh environment, and these dramatically increased the distance over which a potential battle would be fought on the Lunar Surface.

---

30   U.S. Army, 1959.
31   U.S. Army, 1965.
32   U.S. Army, 1959.

Maximum Line of Sight for a Human observer on the Lunar Surface was calculated to be some 8,448 feet (2,574.9 meters) by the 1965 U.S. Army Lunar Surface Weapons Study; and the, Maximum Impact Point of a Horizontal Fired Projectile: 8,190 feet (2,500 meters). This led to a concept of highly distributed form of battle, were individual units of two Soldier-Astronauts would be the basis of tactics, using a variety of weapons in concealed positions engaging with targets at extreme ranges. Given, the ranges possible for direct, and indirect-fire it is likely that a highly distributed type of combat would have been used, with only teams of two riding a thin skinned vehicle designed to afford combatants some means of protection. Each fighting unit searching-out and attacking opposing forces. The concept of battle was likely to be highly mobile, as the Soldier-Astronauts could mount-up and move via surface cars, or low flying vehicles to new positions.

Fundamentally, it was also understood, that the approach to combat and its operations on the Lunar Surface would change according to a two-stage concept development. An initial phase, would be based on known science, developed before arrival on the Moon. A further stage based on discoveries, and technological advancements made during the time spent fighting and operating on the Lunar Surface, would lead to bespoke weapons and combat approaches.

THE HARSH LUNAR SURFACE ENVIRONMENT

Four factors constrain Lunar Surface Combat: (1) Logistical; (2) Technological; (3) Harsh Environment; and, (4) Human Limitations. Immense logistical costs, would have been involved in setting-up and maintaining a Lunar Base, and its military commitment, which was calculated to:

> "spend $6 billion over eight and one-half years ($700 million per year). When one remembers that the federal minimum wage in 1958 was $1.00 per hour, this was a huge sum of money that would have required a significant increase in taxes."[33]

One of the major technology limitations was that any combat operations require the Soldier-Astronauts to wear a Spacesuit. These were highly limited as the earlier Apollo Era Spacesuits: Extra-vehicular Mobility Unit specifications gave 6 hours Primary Life Support, with Backup Life Support of 30 minutes[34]. However, one technological advancement would have been building a Lunar Surface Communications System, which utilized microminiaturized two-way radios installed in the Spacesuit helmets[35]. A Lunar Communications Net would be established[36]. The Communications Net proposal design would allow individual Soldier-Astronauts who were out of sight of an outpost to still communicate. The proposed Communications Net would compensate for the curvature of the Moon, as radios were line-of-sight only, through a series of Lunar Surface Relay Stations.

The decision to use Humans on the Moon as a fighting force, to hold either part or all of it for a country's strategic needs, was due to factor such as capitalizing on how military personnel have superiority, due to their: "pilot training, their tactical abilities, and training with weapons"[37]. A core argument made at the beginning of the Space Warfare Era, was the assumption that a Human

---

33   Borch, 2021.
34   Thomas, 2006.
35   Borch, 2021.
36   U.S. Army, 1959.
37   Remuss, 2011.

pilot on an Orbital Bomber,

> "[possessed] … inherent advantages over machines, particularly in terms of on-the-spot judgment and flexibility."[38]

Using Humans on the Moon was more than compensating for the limitation imposed by the technology of the 1960s, it reflected a strategic-political reality, in terms of Space Warfare Strategic Theory of the mid-1950s. The strategic intent, such as seen with the Soviet example:

> "[going] … to great trouble and expense to permanently man an Orbital Space Station … That effort was clearly made to strengthen their international claim through the symbol of effective occupation."[39]

The Human factor had key limitations in Space, and on the Lunar Surface. Potential distance between targets due to the drastic ballistic changes brought about by the lack of an atmosphere on the Moon, and very low gravity, translated into measurements in terms of several hundreds, or thousands of feet: meters, and in some cases miles: kilometres distance separating a weapon being fired from its intended target. This posed fundamental tactical problems for the Soldier-Astronaut on the ground. The two-week Lunar days and nights, posed significant heat and cold stresses. Sharp light and dark contrasts, and visual space distortions, object size, distance, and shape misperceptions commonly reported by Astronauts in Space, would have had the same issues on the Lunar Surface and this would have presented significant limits to a Soldier-Astronaut's situational awareness, and their ability to judge a target distance, aim or even detect a target at some distance. Operating in complete silence apart from radio communications in the helmet, a typical Soldier-Astronaut was likely limited in how far they could see and feel a potential opponent on the Lunar battlefield.

▲ AIRFIX 1:76 Astronauts.

38 Sambaluk, 2011.
39 Dolman, 2002.

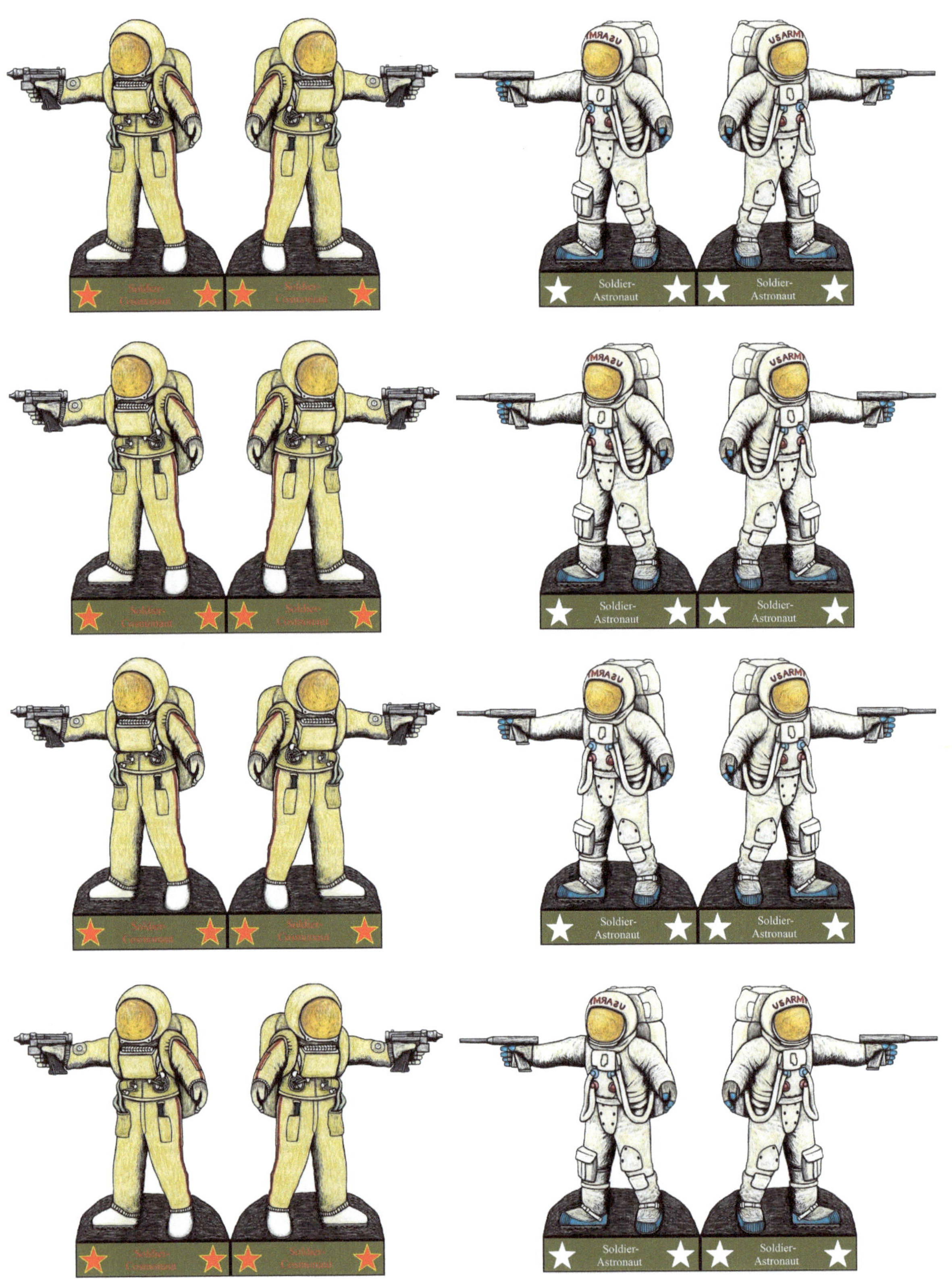

FIGURE PAGE 1 SOLDIER-ASTRONAUT/COSMONAUT INFANTRY

CHAPTER 1: FIGHTING ON THE MOON

INTRODUCTION

Establishing a Lunar Base was seen effectively as claiming and conquering the Moon first. It was intended as a,

> "base, which ultimately would house between ten and twenty personnel, would be the first permanent manned installation on the Moon and, perhaps most importantly, would provide a platform for the Army, if required, to conduct military operations on the Moon."[40]

The question was how could a U.S. Army Taskforce[41][42], that was composed of Soldier-Astronauts defend the Lunar Base? The 1959 U.S. Army Project Horizon Report, noted in regards to weapons and tactics, that:

> "Eventually concepts of military operations on or in the vicinity of the Moon will have to be developed and, from these, supporting requirements for special weapons and equipment will be developed."[43][44]

The 1948 popular science vision of the defensive properties of a Lunar Base, it was seen as:

> "Almost impossible to spot among the maze of surrounding pits, the crater is easy to guard against ground invasion and can be destroyed only by a direct Atom-Bomb hit - a practically impossible feat from our atmosphere-blinded Earth."[45]

There is a strong possibility that the U.S. Army Taskforce deployed to defend the Lunar Base, might likely have been formed and trained as a Pentomic Unit, under the 1950s Pentomic Division concept:

> "Given the Army's development of the Pentomic Division in the 1950s (the 101st Airborne Division became the first Army unit to adopt the Pentomic concept in 1956) for combat on the Atomic battlefield, it is a near certainty that the Army contemplated that it would have Atomic weapons in its new Lunar outpost."[46]

NEW TACTICAL CONCEPTS

To begin with, the Earth's Moon has a total surface area of approximately 37.8 million square kilometres: 14.6 million square miles. A huge area when considering the theoretical maximum walking speed on the Moon is only about five kilometres-per-hour: some three miles[47][48]. While Apollo Astronauts only managed a walking speed of about 2.2 kilometres-per-hour (around a mile only),

40   Borch, 2021.
41   U.S. Army, 1959.
42   Borch, 2021.
43   U.S. Army, 1959.
44   Borch, 2021.
45   Ley, 1948.
46   Borch, 2021.
47   Baker, 2021.
48   Witt, 2014.

due to the Moon's much lower gravity, which gave an Astronaut much less traction on the ground. The Apollo Era Spacesuits were notoriously rigid, and that led to the famous bunny-hopping on the surface of the Moon. The later Boeing 1971 'Moon Buggy' The U.S. Apollo Lunar Roving Vehicle from the later Apollo missions, gave its riders a top speed of 11.2 kilometres-per-hour: 6-7 miles, when it was used, and had a range of 30 kilometres: 18½ miles[49].

The 1965 U.S. Army Lunar Surface Weapons Study argued transition to the Lunar Surface would require a complete redefinition of the enduring features of tactics:

> "It should be kept in mind … that penetration and lethality on the Moon are almost synonymous since penetration of a pressurized vessel on the Moon may be tantamount to defeating it."[50]

Equivalence between penetration and lethality also had another corresponding outcome, namely: the resulting mass of a projectile did not need to be that great. In effect the weight of shot concept in weapons was supplanted by use of small-scale rounds that could have devastating impact and range.

It was feasible for an over the horizon attack to be made from the surface from some 320 miles: 514.9 kilometres away. The 1965 U.S. Army Lunar Surface Weapons Study argued the,

> "approach … [to] … the problem of Space weaponry should recognize the differences in … [Lunar] … conditions"[51].

The major tactics change posed by Lunar conditions, was the curvature of the Moon (its mean radius 1080 miles: 1,737.1 kilometres), meant a Human with an approximate height of six feet: 185 centimetres, was likely to have an unrestricted maximum line of sight some 8,448 feet: 2,574.9 meters away. It was further calculated that a Lunar Surface Personnel Defence Weapon, would have the capability to fire a projectile horizontally, reaching a maximum Point of Impact: Impact Point, some 8,190 feet: 2,500 meters away. It was concluded, that as a result of the high visibility: "A complex set of sights does not therefore appear to be required."[52] High visibility, and long-range effective weaponry would create wide, long-range effective killing zones, which would force both offensive and defensive forces into highly distributed modes of operation dependent on stealth and camouflage in order to escape detection and destruction.

Another major tactics change posed by Lunar conditions, was the slower rotation of the Moon, its 'day' relatively speaking, or the area under light at a given point lasts approximately two weeks from beginning to end, followed by approximately two weeks of darkness, as well periods where there is illumination from Earth-Light. The radical nature of two-weeks of light, followed by two-weeks of darkness could be used as an opportunity to position approaching forces, awaiting the light-time window to launch attacks.

---

49   NASA.
50   U.S. Army, 1965.
51   U.S. Army, 1965.
52   U.S. Army, 1965.

The tactical implications of having weapons available to a combatant with capacity for direct-line of sight fire, and for indirect-fire at more distant targets, such as the opposing combatant's Lunar Base, would likely have created a key operational concept, based on launching operations well-away from the actual position of the Lunar Base, in order to draw-away the potential for attack. The base itself buried, and camouflaged, may have likely led to employment of other traditional deception techniques, such as the development of several dummy-bases, as a means to protect the real base from damage or destruction which if lost could potentially kill the entire base force.

▼ The Lunar Surface Horizon in Relation to the following: (A) Maximum Over the Horizon Range: 320 miles (514.9 kilometres); (B) Maximum Line of Sight: 8,448 feet (2,574.9 meters); (C) Maximum Impact Point of a Horizontal Fired Projectile: 8,190 feet (2,500 meters); and, (D) Maximum Ordinate: the highest point of the trajectory, approximately 80 miles: 128.7 kilometres, above the surface; from (E) Position of a Lunar Surface Combatant.

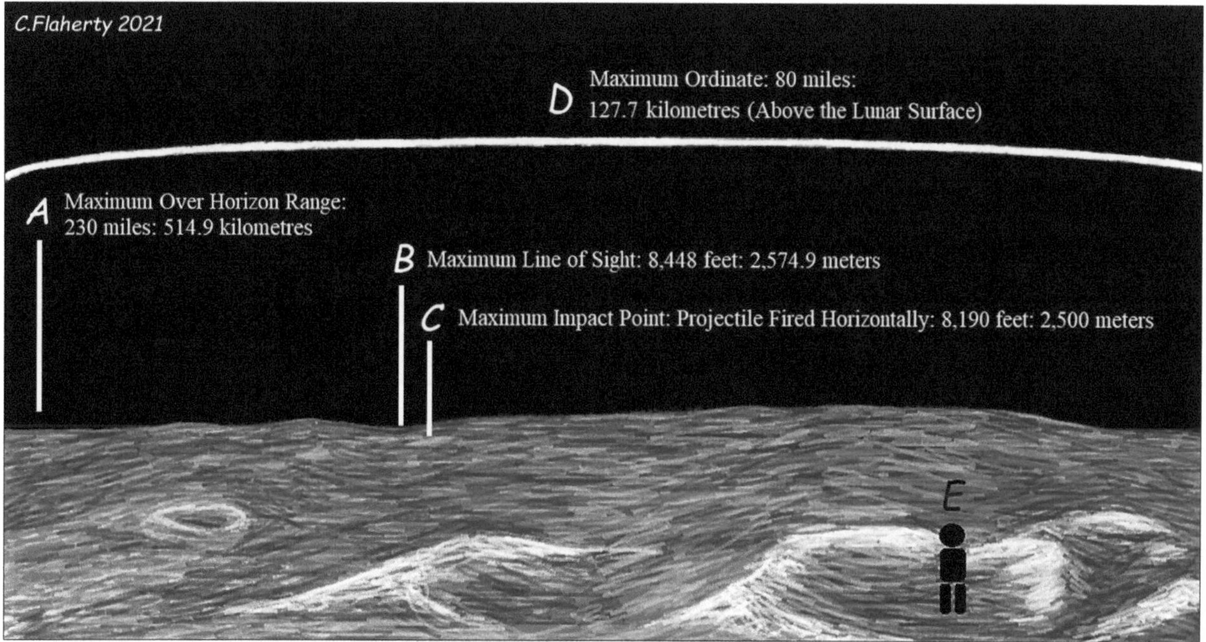

▼ The 1965 U.S. Army Lunar Surface Weapons Study contained an illustration showing two-teamed Soldier-Astronauts of the U.S. Army Taskforce with a low flying vehicle overhead armed with a much larger artillery version of the handgun concepts – possibly a recoilless Gyrojet firing cannon. It appears to have three crew (one was likely a commander – directing the vehicle and surface force). Propelled with two out-lying engine pods with forwards and backwards thrusters, and five more downwards directed thrusters under each pod. Such a craft if designed would have had much the same characteristics as the North American Rockwell One-Person Lunar Flying Unit. The outwards side of each engine pod had U S ARMY in block lettering. The craft Livery was likely white with red lettering following the conventions used by NASA at the time and the need to reflect harsh sunlight from the Lunar day. More than likely critical surface areas might have been covered with gold reflective film – the gold foil seen on the Apollo Lander! Regolith dust build-up would have given some further natural camouflaging.

C.Flaherty 2021
US ARMY
US ARMY

VEHICLES, MOBILITY AND PROTECTION

Vehicles were envisaged for Lunar Base construction, transport, and scouting purposes[53][54], and for protection of combatants[55]. It was thought, "the first defensive personnel weapon … should have a capability of penetrating (at the minimum) thin skinned vehicles."[56] It was also thought initially that vehicles would need to be provided with some type of skin protection. Vehicles would first be thin skinned, advancing to more thicker armour as projectile weapons continued to increase penetrative power. However, the first vehicle envisaged had no protection, and only offered mobility. That was the 'Moon Buggy': "and vehicles of same form will probably soon appear after the first landings (example: NASA's Lunar Roving Vehicle)". [57]

The later electric battery car, the 'Moon Buggy', was the Boeing 1971-72 U.S. Apollo Lunar Roving Vehicle, used for the Apollo 15-16-17 missions. The vehicle gave its two crew riders a reasonable level of Lunar Surface mobility:

▶ Boeing 1971-72 Apollo Lunar Roving Vehicle.			
	TOP SPEED:	11.2 kilometres-per-hour	6-7 miles
	SPECIFIED RANGE:	92 kilometres	57 miles
	Apollo 15 Range:	5 kilometres	3.1 miles
	Apollo 16 Range:	4.5 kilometres	2.7 miles
	Apollo 17 Range:	7.6 kilometres	4.7 miles

The 1967-1969 concept called for a one or two-person rocket-powered Lunar Flying Vehicle-Unit with a range of five to ten kilometres: 6.2 miles[58]. The 1969 Bell Aerosystems One-Person Lunar Flying Unit version, was a standing platform base with four low legs. The craft was designed around their Rocket Belt-Pack that dated from the 1950s, and was marketed to the U.S. Army. This low-power rocket propulsion device allowed an individual to safely travel or leap over small distances. The Astronaut-Pilot stabilized the craft, as they flew it, gripping a pair of handlebar-type controls linked mechanically to twin side-mounted rocket nozzles. The 1969 Bell Aerosystems One-Person Lunar Flying Unit specifications, were:

Actual Sortie Flight Time:	30 minutes	
All Lunar Terrain Ceiling-Height (Above the Surface):	75 feet	22.8 meters
Flying Speed:	70 miles	112.6 kilometres-per-hour
Range:	15 miles	24.1 kilometres

The 1969 North American Rockwell One-Person Lunar Flying Unit version also had a base platform with legs for a seated Astronaut-Pilot with a cluster of small propulsion units directly under the seat. The likelihood that downwards thrusting engine exhaust would excavate-out a hole throwing-up regolith, required a deployable fabric target that unrolled on the Lunar Surface. This was needed for all take-off launch-landing manoeuvres[59].

---

53 U.S. Army, 1959.

54 U.S. Airforce, 1961.

55 U.S. Army, 1965.

56 U.S. Army, 1965.

57 U.S. Army, 1965.

58 Portree, 2013.

59 Portree, 2013.

The 1969 North American Rockwell One-Person Lunar Flying Unit specifications, were:

Maximum Altitude:	2,000 feet		609.6 meters
Range:	4.6 nautical miles	5.2 miles	8.5 kilometres

The North American Rockwell version to increase its range could have add-on spherical auxiliary propellant tanks.

C.Flaherty 2021

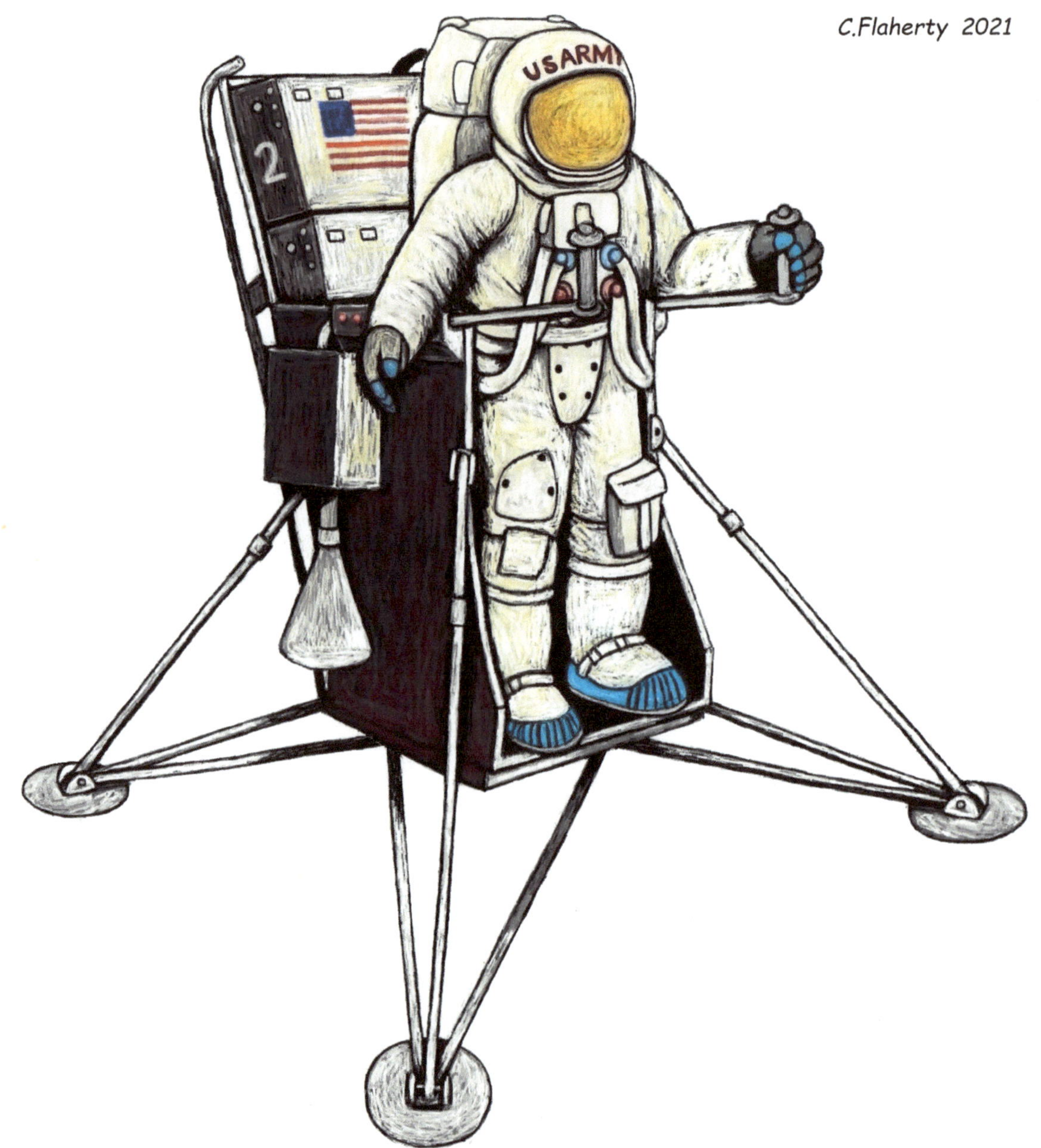

▲ **This illustration of an Astronaut operating a Lunar Surface flying craft is based on one of several concept drawings done by Bell Aerosystems in the 1960s of possible configurations for a One-Person Lunar Flying Unit.**

CHAPTER 2: LUNAR SURFACE PERSONAL DEFENCE WEAPONS OPTIONS

INTRODUCTION

The standard M16 rifle that had in 1964, entered U.S. military service[60], was not considered for potential combat on the Moon. If it had, this might have only been possible with massive modifications to the basic weapon[61]. The 1965 U.S. Army Lunar Surface Weapons Study identified several plausible hand-held presumably smoothbore weapon options, with a much reduced recoil equivalent to the Moon's gravitational field (which is notionally a sixth that of the Earth).

PERSONNEL WEAPONS OPTIONS

Four handheld gun types were proposed to arm a U.S. Army Soldier-Astronaut in the mid-1960s, these Lunar Surface Personnel Defence Weapons, were: (1) Gyrojet Projectile Firing Micro Gun; (2) Sausage Gun (Multi-Barrelled Version of a Gyrojet); (3) Smoothbore Compressed Spring Pistol; and, (4) Self-Protection Pepper-Box Pistol. The longest of these handheld guns was around two feet: 60.96 centimetres in length. The main problem with Lunar Surface Personnel Defence Weapons, was these were either limited to fire their pre-loaded barrels, or had a limited magazine capacity. It appears, the proposed weapons designs were aimed at the need to keep weapon weight at a minimum to reduce rocket transport costs.[62] Combatants were intended to carry multiple weapons at a time, suggesting that a key tactic would be either ride vehicles, or to dig-in, using personal pits, presumably covered by a camouflage net. A method proposed to help maintain Spacesuit temperatures, was the use of, "a reversible white and black umbrella"[63]. This might have doubled as a hide-shelter, which could be camouflaged, or rely on regolith dust built up on the top of the covering to aid concealment.

(1) Gyrojet Projectile Firing Micro Gun

A proposed short single barrel, "spin stabilized micro gun", worked on the Gyrojet projectile principle: firing by electrical ignition a small bullet round packed with its own propellent, that acted like a micro-rocket[64]. It was assumed the Gyrojet projectile firing micro gun would have had sufficient muzzle velocity (calculated to be 3,000 feet-per-second), allowing a projectile fired from the horizontal, reaching its full-distance Impact Point, some 8,190 feet: 2,500 meters away. It was further calculated that the same weapon fired at an angle of 45 degrees, with the Lunar Surface, was understood to greatly increase the maximum range of a projected object (fired at a velocity of 3,000 feet-per-second), to about 320 miles: 514.9 kilometres, with its Maximum Ordinate: the highest point of the trajectory, approximately 80 miles: 128.7 kilometres, above the surface[65].

---

60   Smith, 1983.

61   Mizokami, 2021.

62   U.S. Army, 1965.

63   U.S. Army, 1965.

64   U.S. Army, 1965.

65   U.S. Army, 1965.

(2) Sausage Gun

A multi-barrelled version called a 'sausage' was also envisaged that fired by electrical ignition, a sabot capped flechette with its own propellent case[66]. This weapon, like the Gyrojet projectile firing micro gun would have had a muzzle velocity calculated to be 3,000 feet-per-second, giving it the same range capabilities.

(3) Smoothbore Compressed Spring Pistol

A mid-range weapon envisaged by the 1965 U.S. Army Lunar Surface Weapons Study, was a smoothbore that used a compressed spring to propel a spherical projectile. There was also a 'gas cartridge gun' variation, which relied on compressed gas to fire spherical projectiles. It was envisaged these guns had a muzzle velocity of 1,000 to 1,600 feet-per-second, giving a plausible range of somewhere in the vicinity of 2,624 feet: 800 meters range.

(4) Self-Protection Pepper-Box Pistol

A close-combat weapon envisaged by the 1965 U.S. Army Lunar Surface Weapons Study, was a short-range (estimated to be some three to six feet: 1.8 meters), self-protection pepper-box pistol that relied on a separate single-shot gas blast from a high explosive detonation, "for close-in fighting"[67]. Penetration and lethality equivalence also applied to a combatant wearing a pressurized suit: "it might be sufficient to penetrate a Spacesuit since the suit would then suddenly decompress."[68]

TABLE OF WEAPONS

WEAPON TYPE	MAGAZINE CAPACITY	ANGLE	- RANGES -			
			Miles	Feet	Kilometres	Meters
Self-Protection Pepper-Box Pistol	Single-shot gas blast	Horizontal		3-6		1.8
Gyrojet Projectile Firing Micro Gun	Sabot capped flechette with own propellent case	Horizontal		8,190		2,500
		45 degrees	320		514.9	
		Maximum Ordinate	80		128.7	
Sausage Gun (Multi-Barrelled Version of a Gyrojet)	Sabot capped flechette with own propellent case	Horizontal		8,190		2,500
		45 degrees	320		514.9	
		Maximum Ordinate	80		128.7	
Smoothbore Compressed Spring Pistol	Spherical Projectile	Horizontal		2,624		800
Gas Cartridge Gun	Spherical Projectile	Horizontal		2,624		800

---

66 U.S. Army, 1965.

67 U.S. Army, 1965.

68 U.S. Army, 1965.

▼ A mid-1960s U.S. Army Soldier-Astronaut with U S ARMY in red block letters across the top (above the visor) of the Spacesuit helmet. This is depicted in an illustration in the 1965 U.S. Army Lunar Surface Weapons Study. Typically the U.S. Army, in the 1960s used large white block letter U S ARMY livery on their olive drab painted vehicles. In the case of NASA livery this was white with red lettering USA. Use of white for vehicles and Spacesuits would likely not have changed for U.S. Army use on the Lunar Surface as this was the only way to combat heat during the harsh Lunar day. The following Lunar Surface Personnel Defence Weapons are depicted (the Scale is 0-1-2 feet in length): A. Gyrojet Projectile Firing Micro Gun; B. Smoothbore Compressed Spring Pistol; C. Self-Protection Pepper-Box Pistol; and, D. Sausage Gun (Multi-Barrelled Version of a Gyrojet).

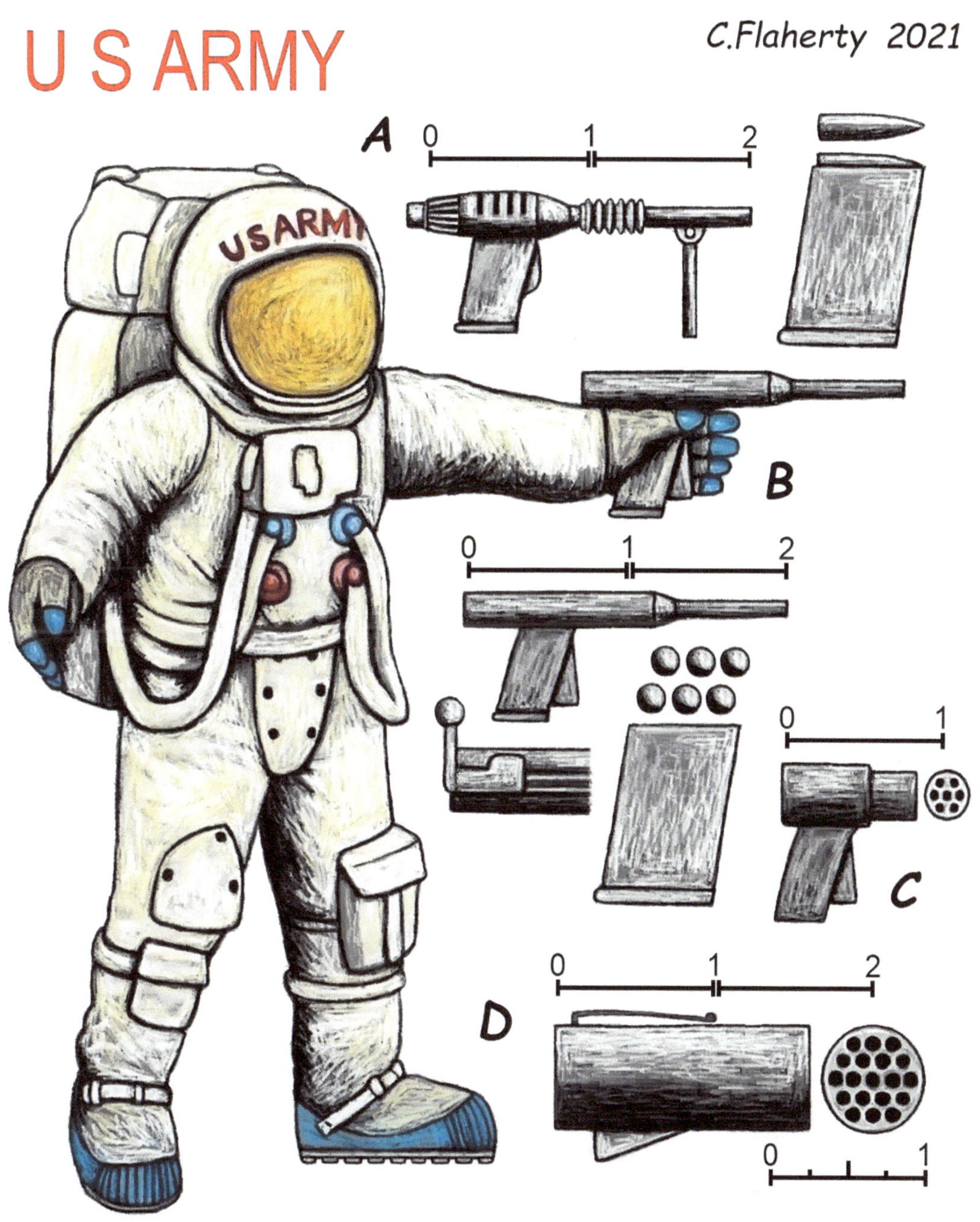

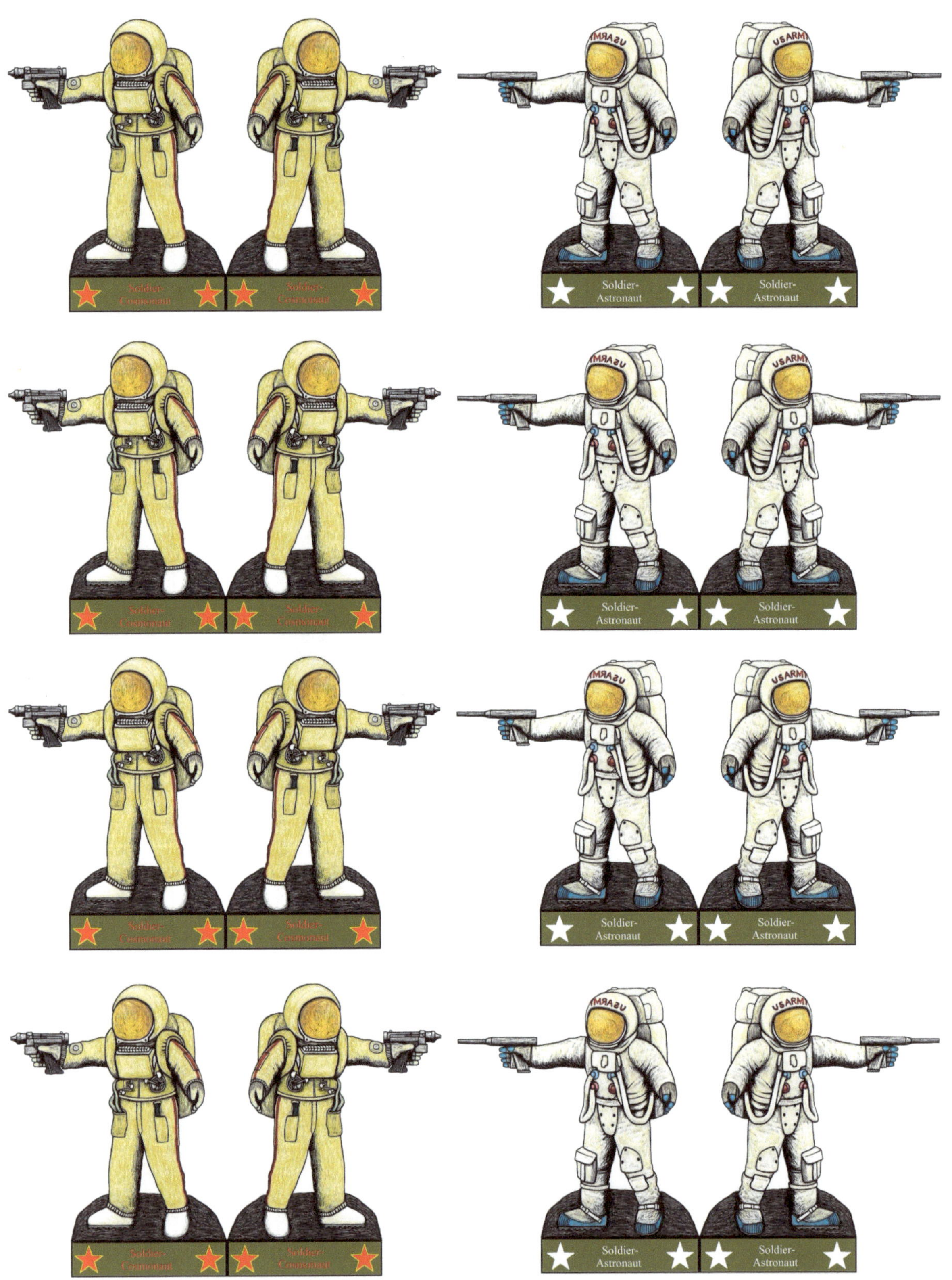

FIGURE PAGE 2 SOLDIER-ASTRONAUT/COSMONAUT INFANTRY

CHAPTER 3: SOVIET EARLY SPACE WARFARE DE-VELOPMENTS (1958-1984)

INTRODUCTION

Little is known about Soviet military concepts in relation to Lunar Surface Combat prior to 1967. In 1958, there was the E-Project (Stage E4), that involved a plan to detonate a small Nuclear charge on the Lunar Surface[69]. Intended as a demonstration of superiority that astronomers across the world could photograph its explosion on film, proving the Soviet Union was capable of landing on the surface of the Moon. The plan never eventuated, and the main Soviet focus in Space Warfare concepts was more on the idea of a Space-Based Orbital Piloted Station. The concept began in late 1964 (however, in 1963 a mock-up of the craft apparently existed), during a design meeting of leading specialists of the OKB-52 Design Bureau, based in Reutov, on the eastern edge of Moscow. The Chief Designer Vladimir Chelomei officially announced the beginning of development of the Orbital Piloted Station, code-named Almaz: Diamond[70]. The main focus was intelligence gathering, based on the view:

> "use of Human eyes and brains seemed promising in Space-Based intelligence. Proponents of manned Space espionage argued that the presence of people in Earth orbit, armed with powerful reconnaissance tools, could provide careful selection of targets and quick reaction to fast-changing developments on the battlefield."[71]

The idea of developing weapons for either the Cosmonaut, or for the Orbital Piloted Station appears to have been much later than the United States, and largely during the post-Outer Space Treaty Era.

1967 ZVEZDA MOON BASE-TRAIN

The Soviets conceived in 1967, a plan to build their Zvezda Moon Base-Train[72]. Envisaged as a set of mobile habitation modules – powered by Atomic batteries and a Nuclear reactor. When parked for any period of time these would be dug-in on the Lunar Surface and covered with regolith for added crew safety. This was achieved as there would be a Train-Rover used,

> "[to] … bulldoze the soil toward the base and another would use a specially built sand-thrower to cover the habitat. A deployable net cage around the module would be used to keep the soil shield in place."[73]

Designers estimated that it would take around 4.3 hours to completely bury the base in sandy soil[74]. The habitation modules were intended to be installed on an eight wheeled chassis, with a separate drive unit. Some sources say several of the modules could have been called for, others

---

69 Gault, 2013.
70 Zak, 2001.
71 Zak, 2001.
72 Zak, 2016.
73 Zak, 2016.
74 Zak, 2016.

only suggest one was used with enough space for six Cosmonauts to work and live inside[75]. This movable base could travel around the Lunar Surface, for exploration or repositioning of the base for some other reason. Similar to the U.S. military planners' concept for their Lunar Base, the base personnel compliment was to have been 9 to 12 Cosmonauts.

A habitation module skin had three layers of protection from micrometeorites, heat and ultraviolet rays. Between the external and internal metal layers was a special Styrofoam core. Designed to be compressible, a habitation module with a reduced length of 4.5 meters: 14.7 feet, extending to 8.6 meters: 28.2 feet long. The habitation module had a diameter of 3.3 meters: 10.8 feet, and weight 18 tons. The module was fitted-out with a control area, laboratory, life-support, medical, dining, and stores locker.

To move the habitation modules, there was a Train-Rover, which worked like a Tug, it had an 8-ton mass and was to have been operated by four Cosmonauts. It was called,

> "the Multipurpose Lunar Engineering Machine, LIM. The three-ton Rover would be used for soil-moving operations and scouting, cargo hauling, and it would also double as a crane and a mobile drilling rig. A telescope-like crane and a drill would be attached to the sides of the cockpit. The Rover would be … equipped with external lighting, TV cameras, and windows."[76]

The Train-Rover was fitted-out the same way as the habitation modules. It had a land drilling unit, and manipulator arm that would have enabled collection of samples of soil without need for the Cosmonauts to venture outside in Spacesuits.

1975 SOVIET ALMAZ SPACE STATION

It was in the mid-to-late 1950s, that the notion of Earth Circumnavigation entered into tactical-strategic thinking with the growing use of satellite surveillance. The ban by a regime of international treaties, largely ended the notion of an Orbital Bomber, or Orbital Battle Station. Nevertheless, Soviet programs, in the early 1970s, initially entertained the notion of the Laser Cannon equipped Polyus Spacecraft[77][78], or the missile-armed Kaskad Space Station housing two Cosmonauts for up to a week[79]. Eventually, an armed Orbital Piloted Station did exist, in direct contravention of the existing treaties: it was the Soviet Cannon Armed Salyut 3 - OPS-2 (Almaz 2), from around 1975; and the post-1975, Soviet OPS-4 armed with two rockets (that did not launch).

The Almaz Space Station was conceived in the early 1960s, and was designed with a crew of three. The Soviets hid their Almaz making these identical to the Salyut Spacecraft. The first Almaz was in 1973, and it was publicly identified as the Salyut-2. The next two Almaz were publicly identified as Salyut-3, and Salyut-5.

The Soviets machine cannon was a specially adapted R-23M Kartech, originally a powerful aircraft

---

75   Zak, 2016.
76   Zak, 2016.
77   Gruntman, 2015.
78   Day, 2010.
79   Day, 2010.

weapon, used on the then Tupolev Tu-22 Blinder Supersonic Bomber[80]. The 23 millimetre cannon was used to arm the Salyut-3: OPS-2 (Almaz-2), around 1975,

> "[it was] … an externally mounted machine gun cannon to defend against American Astronaut attacks."[81]

The Almaz only fired its machine cannon once in 1975. This weapon is understood to have not been recoilless, and its firing had the potential for shock and recoil,

> "to damage the Station but, in the vacuum of Space, those forces raised the possibility that shooting the weapon could send it flying in a dangerously unpredictable fashion … [the solution was] … ignited its … thrusters simultaneously with firing the cannon to counteract the weapon's powerful recoil"[82][83].

1984 SOVIET COSMONAUT LASER PISTOL

The Soviets around 1984, developed a Laser Pistol that used a lamp-cartridge loaded pyrotechnic flash, with a blinding force up to a range of 20 meters: 65 feet[84]. It is generally understood this was designed for close-in combat on a Space Station. The Laser Pistol was intended to 'flash blind' an opponent in close-in fighting, such as during a hostile Spacecraft boarding action. The 1984 Soviet Laser Pistol reflected scenarios,

> "[that led] … Some Russian sources … [to] … characterized the Laser Pistol as an individual self-defence weapon for Cosmonauts in orbit, making an impression that the Soviet Space crews were preparing for shootouts with their enemies inside the Space Station … [it imagines a] … scenario in which American 'Space Troopers' would be able to rendezvous, dock, and break into the pressurized compartment of a Soviet Orbital Facility … the worry prompted … [inventing] … various defences, including the … Laser Pistol … promised to be smaller and lighter than an outright Space cannon … the goal was to make the Laser Pistol as small and light as a normal handgun … Russian sources do not elaborate whether Cosmonauts could use the weapon on a Spacewalk outside the Station. Presumably, they could fire … at the enemy Spacecraft through the window, while staying safely in the pressurized compartment."[85]

80 Zak, 2015.
81 Reesman, 2020.
82 Zak, 2015.
83 Trevithick, 2021.
84 Zak, 2018.
85 Zak, 2018.

▲ A Russian 1967 Lunar Surface Krechet-94 Spacesuit. The Cosmonaut is using a 1984 Soviet Space Station Defence Laser Pistol.

CHAPTER 4: LUNAR SURFACE WARGAMING RULES

INTRODUCTION TO THE DISTRIBUTED BATTLE MODEL

The basic concept is that battles are fought using distributed units at great distance from each other. This means not all figures or models are present on the table. A typical battle involves a Lead Unit that actually encounters an opponent on the RED LINE: a borderline on the Lunar Surface demarking two territorial claims, which then draws other units into supporting roles, or launching their own attacks from their positions against a common target.

The high effectiveness of firepower – any type of penetration can have a catastrophic effect on the Lunar Surface, and most of the weapons fire is being undertaken as random long range high-arching shots, this can have extensive area effect. This forces two-person units to stay separate, and only appear when these need to expose themselves (come-out from concealment) to make an attack.

The following set of rules are intended for play using paper cut-out figures provided in this book. The AIRFIX 1/76 Astronauts are suggested for these rules, as are other models, and figures that would also be usable listed in the Annex list.

GAME RECYCLING

These wargaming rules are based on the concept of recycling units. At the beginning of a game a recycle-target is set for each of the unit types indicating how many times a unit can be recycled through. A typical army used in a game will consist of the following:

TROOP TYPES	COMPOSITION	NUMBER	RECYCLED
Soldier-Astronaut Team:	A unit of two figures individually or together on a scenic base with a Lunar Roving Vehicle.	THREE	THREE TIMES
Lunar Flying Vehicle-Unit:	Model and crew figure.	ONE	TWO TIMES

A unit in these rules is a squad (stand of two figures), on foot with a model Lunar Roving Vehicle.

A flying Lunar Vehicle-Unit and its pilot is also an effective unit.

A recycle-replacement unit arrives, when a unit is extinguished, on the table edge and awaits orders.

GROUND SCALE USED

The ground scale is: 1 centimetre is equal to 10 meters. It is used for movement and firing purposes. It does not apply to unit or figure basing (which like the figure size is purely representational). The base represents the area that the figure is moving around, and for the purposes of calculating range these are done unit base edge to opposing unit base edge.

EXPERIENCE STATUS

A commander, or unit is given one of two ratings: this is determined by a D6 dice: 1-2-3 for TRAINED; or, 4-5-6 for REGULAR (all units used must have their EXPERIENCE STATUS established at the start of the game):

TRAINED	A recently deployed Soldier-Astronaut with no Lunar Combat Experience.
REGULARS	Highly experienced Soldier-Astronaut with likely Lunar Combat Experience.

UNIT STAMINA DECLARATIONS

Each unit is given a STAMINA at the beginning of a game which reduces, or increases as it battles-away during the game (this STAMINA is used to determine a unit's STATUS (see (6) UNIT STATUS ASSESSMENTS) that is determined at the end of a player's game turn:

UNIT TYPE	STAMINA
TRAINED	20
REGULARS	24

A PLAYER'S GAME TURN PHASES

In general, players take alternating turns with nine phases:

(1) DETECTION (THE PICKET TEST) RULES: ARE ONLY USED TO BEGIN THE GAME
(2) ORDERS
(3) TIME INTERVALS AND MOVEMENT RATES
(4) WEAPON FIRE RULES
(5) HAND-TO-HAND COMBAT SCORING
(6) UNIT STATUS ASSESSMENTS
(7) DISORDERED UNIT AND RALLY ORDER
(8) BROKEN UNITS
(9) GRID SQUARES AND METEOR STRIKES

The Hand-to-Hand Combat phase takes place where players resolve the bout concurrently. Units fired-on test to resolve their STAMINA/STATUS, after all firing is completed.

(1) DETECTION (THE PICKET TEST) RULES

Detection is the starting phase in the first player's game turn. Each player has very limited understanding of where their opponent forces are likely to be on, or under the Lunar Surface – until any actual battle starts. Above ground reconnaissance from fly-overs by a Lunar Flying Vehicle-Unit or from an orbiting station gives only a limited picture of the possible position of military assets, and both sides make extensive use of dummy positions in order to confuse an opponent. On the ground, notwithstanding that the Maximum Line of Sight for a Human observer on the Lunar Surface was calculated to be some 8,448 feet (2,574.9 meters), overall situational awareness is low. The following rules are used to test where and when a Lead Unit operating as a Picket is able to identify the position of an opponent.

Detection Rules are based on a player, undertaking a Picket Test by their Lead Unit. The Picket Test is based on the following factors: (1) Rated Level of Observation; and, (2) Picket Reaction.

The game begins with the Picket (Lead Unit) testing with a D6 dice-role to see if they spot approaching troops on the RED LINE: borderline that divides the combatant's territories, to a depth of 80 centimetres arc of their position (as it is assumed that there is unobstructed view for around 800 meters). The 80 centimetres distance also represents the Horizontal range of a weapon. The Picket reactions:

TRAINED	NOT SO OBSERVANT:	Spot approaching troops on a D6 dice score:	5-6
REGULARS	VIGILANT:	Spot approaching troops on a D6 dice score:	1-2-3-4

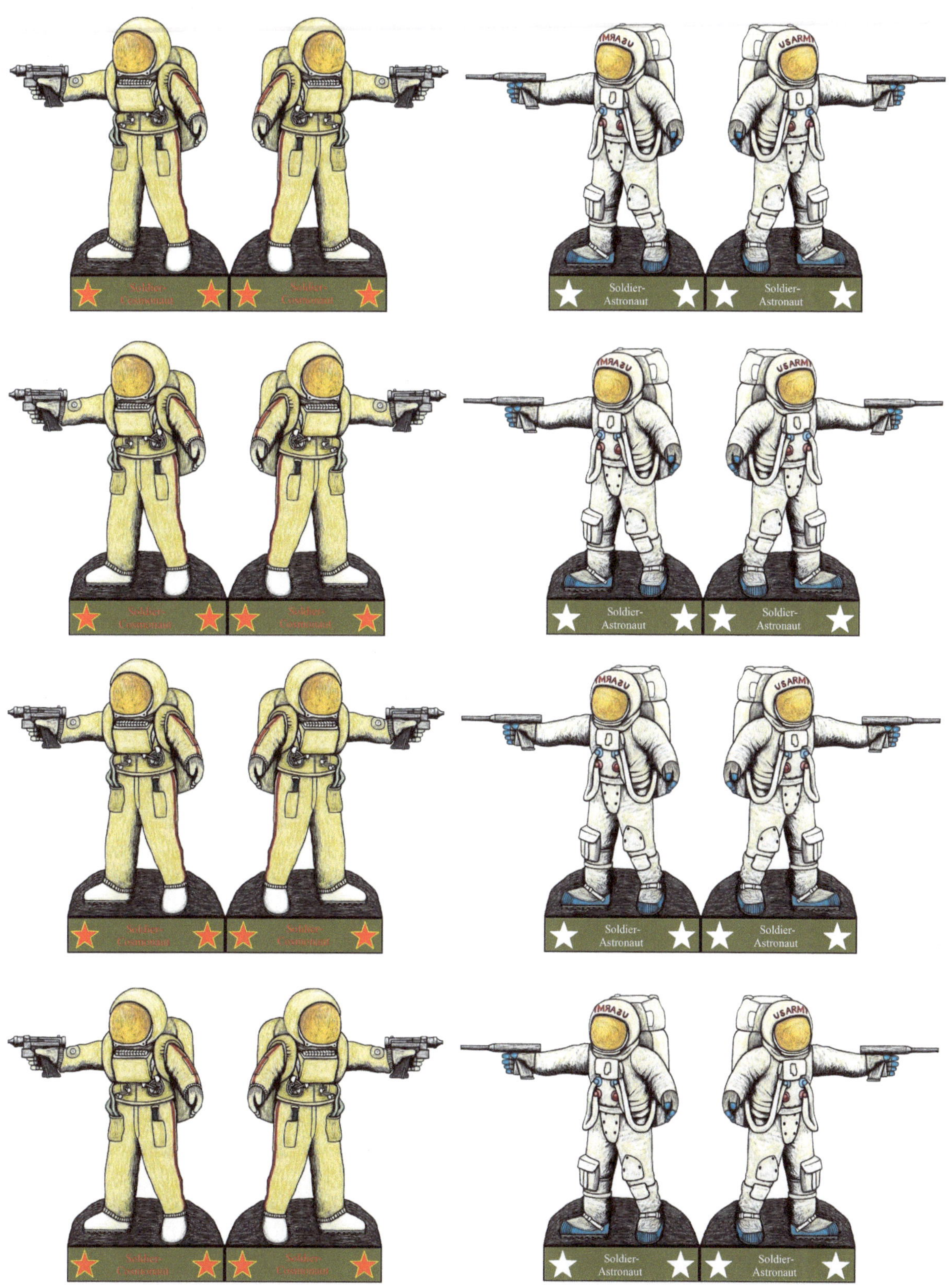

FIGURE PAGE 3 SOLDIER-ASTRONAUT/COSMONAUT INFANTRY

If the Picket fails to see anything, or their reaction is to discount what they see, the resulting report effects the type of order that a Space Sub-Commander can give. If the Picket sees an approaching unit, a further test is taken using a D6 dice role:

1-2-3	NOT SO OBSERVANT Picket see the approaching force, but DISCOUNTS – DOES NOT ACT
4-5-6	NOT SO OBSERVANT Picket see the approaching force and REACTS
1-2-3	VIGILANT Picket see the approaching force, but DISCOUNTS – DOES NOT ACT
4-5-6	VIGILANT Picket see the approaching force and REACTS

If the Picket (sees/reacts), a further dice role is thrown, to see what they will do? That is, they see an approaching enemy, but how do they react to this event:

1-2-3-4-5	The Picket successfully sends-out a warning to the Space Sub-Commander.
6	Considered a blunder. The Picket panics and does not act.

An alternative Picket can be a Lunar Flying Vehicle-Unit (the example used here is the 1969 Bell Aerosystems One-Person Lunar Flying Unit). The craft had a much greater rate of movement over a five minute interval that a walking: bunny-hopping Soldier-Astronaut Infantryman, or a Lunar Roving Vehicle. However, its Actual Sortie Flight Time was restricted to 30 minutes. Used for a reconnaissance flyover, at the start of the first player's game turn (the flyover can also be done again every five game turns: if a Commander elects to do so, as they need more intelligence). The Bell craft had a fairly low flying height above Lunar Surface terrain of 75 feet: 22.8 meters. This limits the reconnaissance information that can be gained to an 80 centimetres wide corridor along the Lunar Flying Vehicle-Unit line-of-flight, the length of the table – along the RED LINE.

The craft flies over the table (from one-end to the other– along the RED LINE: borderline that divides the combatant's territories). Its movement is 933 centimetres. In terms of it seeing any-thing, the Picket Test is used. The pilot's rating is also determined at the start of the game as either TRAINED or REGULAR. A Picket Test is made in each grid square (see (9) GRID SQUARES). If multiple units are seen – all can be identified and fired-on by corresponding units who are ordered to do so. Once a unit fires its position is known to an opponent.

An opponent unit can be ordered to fire-up at a Lunar Flying Vehicle-Unit. A HIT on a craft forces it to leave the area (see (4.3) FIRING AT A MOVING VEHICLE). This immediately alerts the Sub-Space Commander (or a Space Commander) to the presence of this enemy unit (and its likely location): and an order can be given to the closest surface unit – to respond such as fire at it! This is all the information to be had from the flyover as the pilot will need to bug-out as they are taking fire!

(2) ORDERS

If the Space Sub-Commander, or Space Commander is getting no reaction from the Picket (Lead Unit), and a unit is fired-on, or contacted by an enemy, then all the units go into Extreme Caution Mode: effectively Battlefield Blind, only defensive actions are taken by a unit (operating without an order until the next game turn), and all unit movements (if this occurs) is a quarter of the normal speed, depending on the terrain (see (3) TIME INTERVALS AND MOVEMENT RATES).

The initial force involved in a battle is the Lead Unit (Picket), and two other units: a total of three under a local Space Sub-Commander, who then has a higher-level Space Commander. The Space Commander can activate all the Moon-Based, and Orbital Military Forces at their disposal and bring these into the battle: from the reserve force on the Intermediate Orbiting Space Sta-

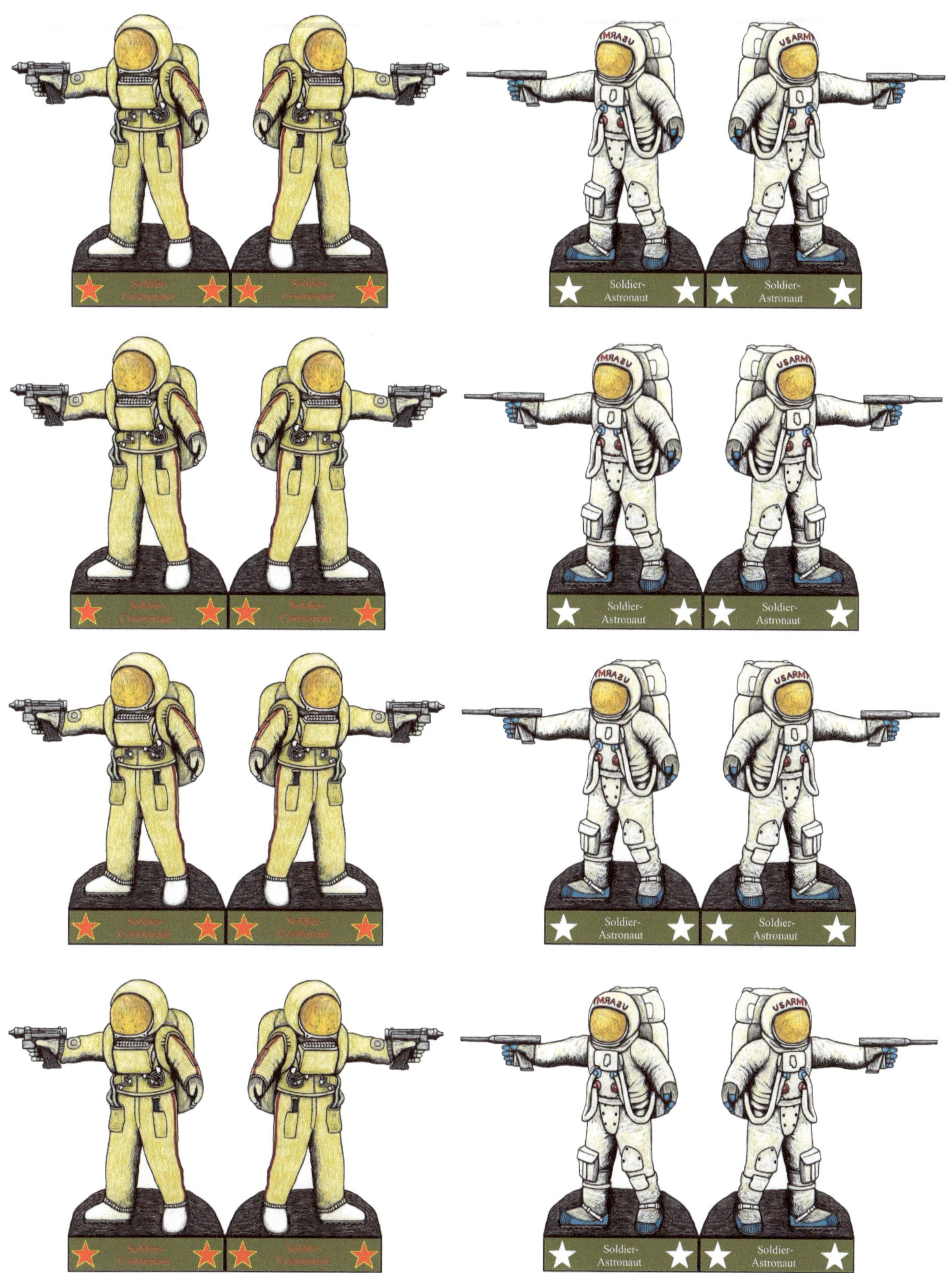

FIGURE PAGE 4 SOLDIER-ASTRONAUT/COSMONAUT INFANTRY

tion. Commanders are given a Command Value, which is determined by a D6 dice: 1-2-3 for TRAINED; or, 4-5-6 for REGULAR.

▶ Like the Soldier-Astronauts, the Commanders are either TRAINED or REGULAR, which effects their Command Value:

COMMAND LEVEL	COMMAND VALUE	
SPACE COMMANDER	TRAINED	7
	REGULAR	8
SPACE SUB-COMMANDER	TRAINED	7
	REGULAR	8

Orders begin with the Space Sub-Commander, who has direct control of three units: that are each initially located in one of the table grid squares (see (9) GRID SQUARES). The Space Sub-Commander can elect after the third game-turn if they want to engage the Space Commander. To do so the Space Sub-Commander must test to see if this is successful or not. Giving orders to a unit, or transferring command from the Space Sub-Commander to the Space Commander, a player uses two D6 dice. The roll-score cannot be higher than the Commanding officers' Command Value if they want to give a successful order. If the score is less than, or equal to the Command Value then a successful order can be given. If the roll-score is over the Command Value, and the following modifiers do not effect the result, no order can be given:

TRAINED	A recently deployed Soldier-Astronaut with no Lunar Combat Experience.	-1
REGULARS	Highly experienced Soldier-Astronaut with likely Lunar Combat Experience.	-2

(1.1) UNIT WITHOUT ORDERS

A unit without orders cannot move or take any action. If attacked it may defend itself, and it can engage in Hand-to-Hand Combat as a DISORDERED unit. Players can adopt a wild-card scenario: a units' response is dictated by a D6 dice role; and the unit undertakes one of the following response if attacked:

1-2-3	STAY, DEFEND AND FIRES	Stays in location, adopts a defensive position, and fires at the oncoming attacker.
4	CHARGES (does not need to be in range)	Moves in the direction of the attacker without firing. If it makes contact initiates Hand-to-Hand Combat.
5	BROKEN	Moves directly away from the attacker towards its own side. Must receive a RALLY order.
6	SURRENDERS	Unit is removed from the table. This only effects the unit on the table, and not its recycle-replacement.

A Charge order adds an extra 5 centimetres to a unit's range. These are only conducted on foot - so it is extra vigorous bunny-hopping for the Soldier-Astronauts! If a unit Blunders and charges and does not make contact it is caught in the open and it suffers a -2 to its STAMINA if it is HIT. One of the major problems effecting a Lunar Surface battleplan would be a break-down of the Lunar Surface Communications System. The system utilizes microminiaturized two-way radios installed in the Spacesuit helmets. Allowing individual Soldier-Astronauts who were out of sight of an outpost to still communicate. As radios are line-of-sight only, and can be blocked by the curvature of the Moon, communications take place through a series of Lunar Surface Relay Stations. A critical problem during bombardment of an area, is that a Relay Station can be damaged, cutting-off radio communications, this halts orders being sent or received. It is suggested, where there has been recent area fire, or a meteor hit in a grid square (see (9) GRID SQUARES), that a Communications Test is taken. A dice role of 5-6 will mean Communications Failure for the next two turns for a player (awaiting a repair to take place).

Reverse Side of Lunar Rover

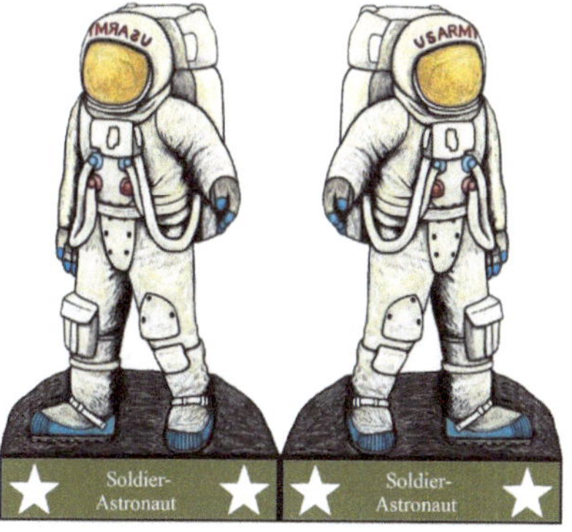

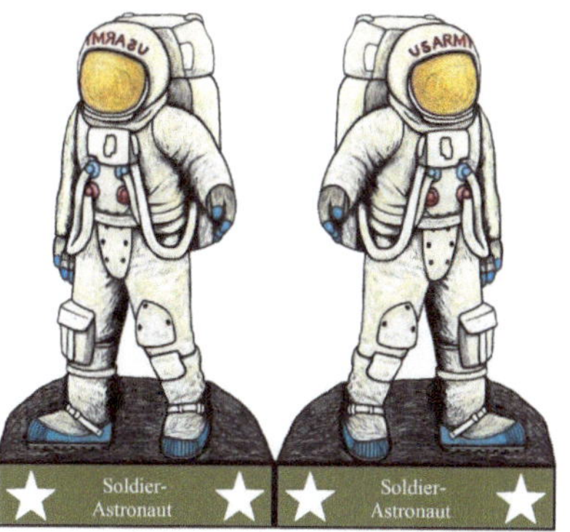

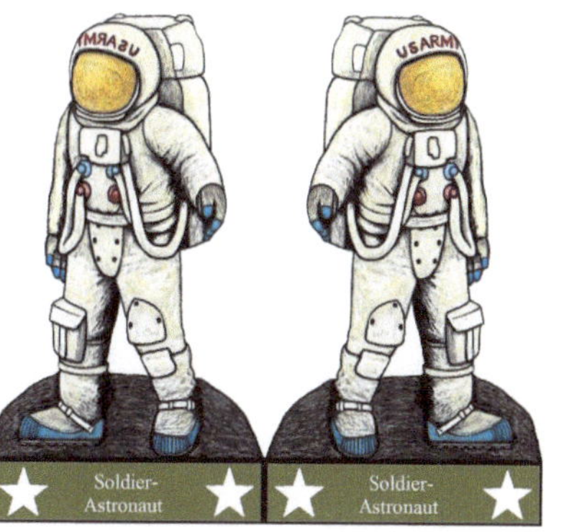

C.Flaherty 2021

FIGURE PAGE 5 SOLDIER-ASTRONAUT ROVER TEAM

(1.2) UNIT WITH ORDERS

For each unit to act it must receive an order. A successful order allows Commanders options to set the direction by nominating the position on the table a unit will move to, and one of several tactical options available to a unit. An order normally lasts for a player's game turn. An order can also be issued for multiple game turns, until the order is countermanded.

UNIT GIVEN AN ORDER TO:	ACTION	EFFECTIVENESS	CONTROL FACTOR
MOVE ORDER ON FOOT / DRIVE A VEHICLE	Standard movement formation on foot or in a vehicle.	Any unit caught ON THE MOVE when fired on will receive heavy casualties.	LOW
FIRE-AND-MOVE ORDER	Staggered sub-units that leap-frog. One moves, as the alternate sub-unit fires.	Offers greater cover during an attack. Keeps opponent under fire. Reduces casualties. However, unit is exposed, divided and isolated.	LOW
LINE-ATTACK ORDER	Single line formation to advance/charge against an opponent.	Reduces formation depth and its casualties.	HIGH
FIRE LINE ORDER	Single static line formation to fire at an opponent.	Reduces formation depth to reduce casualties.	HIGH
DIG-IN DEFENSIVE POSITION ORDER	Static defendable place.	Offering greater protection from fire.	HIGH

Choice of tactics have an impact on the CONTROL FACTOR which is linked to the UNIT'S EFFECTIVENESS. This is used as a factor in calculating a unit's STATUS (see EXPERIENCE STATUS), and its STAMINA (see (6) UNIT STATUS ASSESSMENTS).

(3) TIME INTERVALS AND MOVEMENT RATES

The Time Interval used in these rules for a player's game turn are five minute intervals. The whole battle period itself is limited by the earlier Apollo Era Spacesuits: Extravehicular Mobility Unit that gave 6 hours Primary Life Support, with Backup Life Support of 30 minutes. Apollo Era Astronauts only managed a walking: bunny-hopping speed of about 2.2 kilometres-per-hour (around a mile only). The following movement rates are used:

TYPE	SPEEDS		
Scale: 1 centimetre = 10 meters	WALKING	DRIVING	FLYING
SOLDIER-ASTRONAUT INFANTRY	18 centimetres		
LUNAR ROVING VEHICLE		58 centimetres	
LUNAR FLYING VEHICLE-UNIT			933 centimetres

In addition to the basic movement distances, these are modified by the following terrain categories:

TERRAIN TYPE	SOLDIER-ASTRONAUT INFANTRY	LUNAR ROVING VEHICLE	LUNAR FLYING VEHICLE-UNIT
OPEN GROUND PLATEAU	Standard Movement	Standard Movement	Standard Movement
BROKEN GROUND, OBSTACLES OR CRATERED	Movement Quartered	Movement Halved	Standard Movement
BUILDING – LUNAR BASE AREA	Movement Quartered	BLOCKED	Standard Movement

Reverse Side of Lunar Rover

FIGURE PAGE 6 SOLDIER-ASTRONAUT ROVER TEAM

(4) WEAPON FIRE RULES

Generally, each unit is understood to have four weapons options (the unit carries all of these weapons, and will be ordered as to which one is used), with the following ranges and capabilities:

WEAPON TYPE	MAGAZINE CAPACITY	ANGLE	RANGE (Meters)	DISTANCE (Centimetres)
Gyrojet Projectile Firing Micro Gun	Sabot capped flechette with own propellent case	Horizontal	2,500	250
		45 degrees	514.9	50
		Maximum Ordinate	128.7	13
Sausage Gun (Multi-Barrelled Version of a Gyrojet)	Sabot capped flechette with own propellent case	Horizontal	2,500	250
		45 degrees	514.9	50
		Maximum Ordinate	128.7	13
Smoothbore Compressed Spring Pistol or Gas Cartridge Gun	Spherical Projectile	Horizontal	800	80
Self-Protection Pepper-Box Pistol	Single-shot gas blast	Horizontal	1.8	Point Blank (Bases Touching)

(4.1) HORIZONTAL FIRING

If a Lead Unit (Picket) successfully sees/reacts to an enemy unit, it can be ordered to fire at it. In order for a unit to fire Horizontally: the full-distance from its base edge must be clear of obstructions. Two D6 dice roles are used to determine a HIT, or HITS:

TRAINED FIRING HORIZONTALLY	Two dice to HIT	5-6
REGULARS FIRING HORIZONTALLY	Two dice to HIT	4-5-6

The main difference between Soldier-Astronaut Infantry fire is the effectiveness of these who are either TRAINED or REGULARS. It is expected that a REGULAR will have a higher-better fire rate. These troops can be given an extra dice re-role (in addition to their two D6 initial roles) when firing at Horizontal range only.

EXPLANATION: The main limitation on the ability of a Soldier-Astronaut to effectively HIT their target is the effect experienced in Space, and on the Moon's Surface on Human eyesight – which is known to have problems. This combined with the potential distance between targets measured in terms of several hundreds, or thousands of feet: meters, and in some cases miles: kilometres distance, means that it is actually difficult to see a target. A target is potentially obscured by sharp light and dark contrasts, and visual space distortions, object size, distance, and shape misperceptions - all commonly reported by Astronauts in Space.

A unit can only Horizontal fire at a target where there is no line-of-sight obstructions (in any other circumstances – such as a crater edge separating units, then INDIRECT-FIRE must be attempted).

(4.2) INDIRECT-FIRE RULES AND AREA EFFECT RULES

A unit can be ordered to engage in long-range firing a weapon at 45 degrees, or Maximum Ordinate: the highest point of the trajectory, and this type of weapon fire converts into INDIRECT-FIRE due to Lunar Surface Terrain or the Moon's curvature.

The range for INDIRECT-FIRE varies: (1) A weapon fired at an angle of 45 degrees has a greater range: 50 centimetres; whereas, (2) A weapon fired at its Maximum Ordinate: the highest point of the trajectory, has the shortest range: 13 centimetres, from the unit's base edge.

Reverse Side of Lunar Rover

FIGURE PAGE 7 SOLDIER-COSMONAUT ROVER TEAM

The DEAD-GROUND distance/area is where a projectile cannot land, due to fire at a high-arc trajectory (effectively lobbing their shots upon a target). Up to two D6 dice roles are allotted to a unit when it uses INDIRECT-FIRE:

FIRING ORDER	DEAD-GROUND & RANGES (Centimetres):		ROLE	SCORE
FIRING AT 45 DEGREES	NIL (0-50)	50	Two dice to HIT	5-6
FIRING AT MAXIMUM ORDINATE	NIL (0-13)	13	One dice to HIT	6

EXPLANATION: The reason why fire at Maximum Ordinate has less chance of hitting a target, is due to its spread of shot, being lesser at a closer range, than at a greater range where an impact area is larger.

INDIRECT-FIRE: is where the weapon is being fired at an angle of 45 degrees, or its Maximum Ordinate: the highest point of the trajectory, will be largely treated as not an aimed-shot, but falling within an area – that could be effected. The fire rules presented here are based on an area of the game table being selected. Weapons fired at a high arc over the Lunar Surface toward a target in effect becomes an area that is under attack. This could be a spread-out Lunar Base, or could be a player deciding on long-range fire with the view of potentially HITTING an opponent's forces without direct knowledge of their exact position – somewhat like 'Battleships' being played.

A player ordering INDIRECT-FIRE designates a Target-Point, and Surrounding Area that is being attacked. This is calculated as a circular zone which is estimated (for the purposes of these rules), to be:

Target Point:	All units within 5 centimetres range of the Target Point.
Surrounding Area:	All units within 10 centimetres range of the Target Point.

The attacking player then roles a D6 dice to determine the effectiveness of the barrage, first for the Target Point, and then for the Surrounding Area:

1	Unit suffers major casualties, and is eliminated.
2-3	Unit is DISORDERED and it suffers: '-1' deduction from its STAMINA.
4-5-6	Unit is DISORDERED only.

If HITS are recorded this identifies to the attacking commander the whereabouts of opposing units. This information can then be used to direct other unit's fire onto this location.

(4.3) FIRING AT A MOVING VEHICLE

A unit may fire at a moving vehicle, such as a Lunar Rover, or Lunar Flying Vehicle-Unit. A D6 dice role is used to determine a HIT or not. While neither offer much protection, and a Lunar Flying Vehicle-Unit has a maximum ceiling-height (over all types of Lunar Surface terrain) of only 75 feet: 22.8 meters; the vehicle's speed likely protects it from actual damage from fire – it is hard to hit!

(4.4) FIRE-EFFECT RULES

Firing is calculated by throwing a D6 dice for each unit. If HITS are recorded, the effect on the receiving unit is represented by a potential change in its STATUS, by reducing its STAMINA (see (6) UNIT STATUS ASSESSMENTS) that is determined at the end of a player's game turn.

(5) HAND-TO-HAND COMBAT SCORING

Hand-to-Hand Combat occurs where a unit has been ordered to attack another unit – coming into direct contact. This is represented by both units touching bases.

Reverse Side of Lunar Rover

C.Flaherty 2021

FIGURE PAGE 8 SOLDIER-COSMONAUT ROVER TEAM

The close-in point blank range of the self-protection pepper-box pistol was intended as a prelude to hand-to-hand fighting between Soldier-Astronauts. A defending unit if attacked are allowed to discharge their pistols, a HIT/HITS is recorded against the attacking unit if they role a 6, using two D6 dice.

Generally speaking, post-WW2 Soldiers reached a high-level competency in terms of their individual combat skill, not only in rapid firing of small arms, but in bayonet and Hand-to-Hand Combat (based on experience in the Korean, or Viet Nam Wars). Special training Hand-to-Hand Combat, and boxing were well established, along with a growing interest in Eastern Martial Arts Traditions in the 1960s. The ethos of close-quarter fighting with knives was equally well-known in post-WW2 armies.

Translating Hand-to-Hand Combat to a low gravity environment on the Lunar Surface wearing a Spacesuit leads to each of the combatants fighting in one-sixth gravity, where Soldier-Astronauts grappling each other's suits attempting to compromise these – causing a rip, or damaging hoses leading in-out of the Life Support Unit leading to a catastrophic decompression of the suit killing the wearer.

All Hand-to-Hand Combat is calculated by throwing two D6 dice for each unit. The side with the highest number of HITS wins the bout. The Hand-to-Hand Combat portion of the game involves both players units resolving the combat result in the same phase. Each unit is represented by two D6 dice for Hand-to-Hand Combat to see if a HIT/HITS are made:

TARGET UNIT DECLARED AT ORDERS PHASE	
SUCCESSFUL ORDER GIVEN. THE UNIT MOVES INTO CONTACT WITH THEIR TARGET	
DEFENDER	Fires self-protection pepper-box pistol. Roles for casualties inflicted on the ATTACKER.
ATTACKER	Makes the First Role. Roles for casualties inflicted on the DEFENDER.
DEFENDER	Roles for casualties inflicted on the ATTACKER.
WINNER DECLARED	
LOSER MUST TEST	

The unit receiving the most HITS is the loser. The losing unit must use a D6 dice to determine what the unit will do:

SCORE	STATUS	ACTION/MODIFICATIONS	
5-6	OPERATIONAL	Stays and fights-on.	-1 Modification to its next result.
4	DISORDERED	Stays and fights-on.	-2 Modification to its next result.
3	BROKEN	Unit is not able to fight and is fleeing the battlefield. Must be given a RALLY order to stop, or it will be lost once it leaves the table.	
1-2	SURRENDERS	Unit is removed from the table. This only effects the unit on the table, and not its recycle-replacement.	

Once two units are locked in Hand-to-Hand Combat, they stay locked-together. The bout continues into the next player's game turn.

(6) UNIT STATUS ASSESSMENTS

Under these rules a unit has one of four levels of STATUS (and a corresponding STAMINA level):

STATUS	EXPLANATION	STAMINA
OPERATIONAL	Standard STATUS for a unit. Ready for battle.	FULL-STAMINA
DISORDERED	Unit has reduced capacity to fight.	HALF-STAMINA
BROKEN	Unit is not able to fight and is fleeing.	BELOW HALF- STAMINA
SURRENDERS	Unit is removed from the table.	NIL

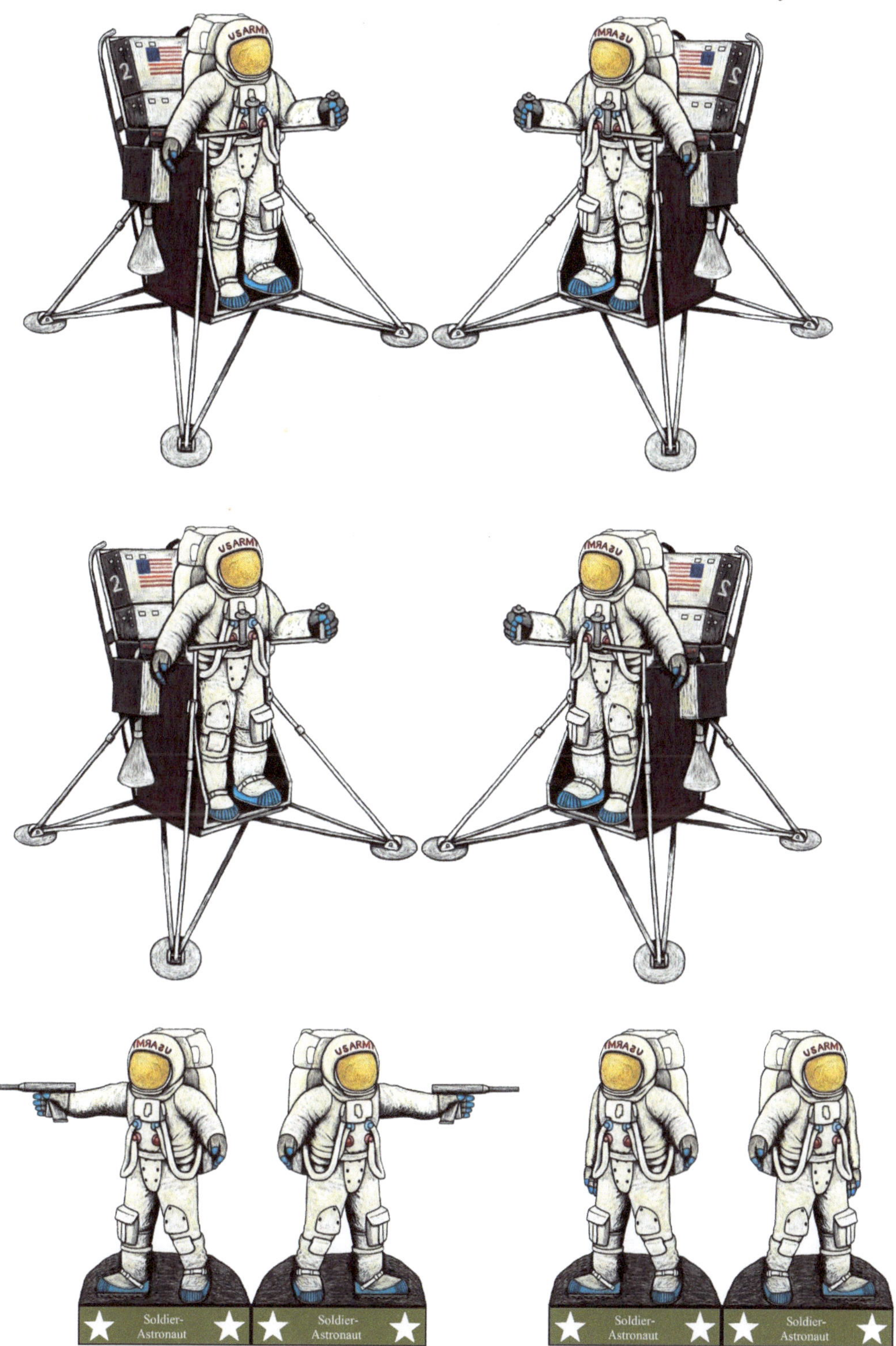

FIGURE PAGE 9 SOLDIER-ASTRONAUT FLYER

All units, on the table or awaiting recycle-replacement units have OPERATIONAL STATUS. Changes in STATUS only occur as a result of the combat phases: such as having been fired-on.

The following additions and subtractions are made from the unit's STAMINA for TRAINED (20 Value: 10 Half-Value) or REGULARS (24 Value: 12 Half-Value):

USING TACTICS WITH HIGH CONTROL FACTOR	+1
DUG-IN	+2
USING TACTICS WITH LOW CONTROL FACTOR	-1
TAKEN FIRE CASUALTIES	-2
LOST A HAND-TO-HAND ATTACK	-2
DISORDERED	-3
BROKEN	-4

EXAMPLE: If a REGULAR unit has full STAMINA (24), is using High Control Factor Tactics (+1), is Dug-in (+2), has Taken Fire Casualties (-2); lost Hand-to-Hand (-2), is DISORDERED (-3), its final STAMINA at the end of the game turn is 20 Value. The reduced STAMINA is recorded on a Player's Table of Results.

If a unit STAMINA is reduced to half (i.e. 12 for a REGULAR unit). The Unit becomes DISORDERED (see (7) DISORDERED UNIT AND RALLY ORDER).

If the unit has less than half its original STAMINA it becomes BROKEN (see (8) BROKEN UNITS AND RALLY ORDER).

A unit that runs out of STAMINA is extinguished and removed from the table. This allows a recycled unit to arrive on the table edge and await its orders.

(7) DISORDERED UNIT AND RALLY ORDER

A unit remains DISORDERED till it is given a successful RALLY order. It will stay a DISORDERED unit, until the next turn where a successful order can make it OPERATIONAL. If the order is not successful it stays DISORDERED till the next turn.

(8) BROKEN UNITS AND RALLY ORDER

A unit that is BROKEN keeps withdrawing towards the nearest edge of the table till it receives a successful RALLY order and returns to DISORDERED. It stops in that location and collects itself. It can take no other actions until the next game turn. It will stay a DISORDERED unit, until the next turn where a successful order can make it OPERATIONAL. If it leaves the table-top it is lost. This rule does not affect its recycle-replacement unit.

(9) GRID SQUARES AND METEOR STRIKES

The Lunar Surface is randomly struck by meteors. Every three game turns (from the start of the game) players need to dice for a potential meteor impact. The playing field is divided into six grid squares, numbered 1-6 (the impact is determined by a D6 dice role):

1	2	3
4	5	6

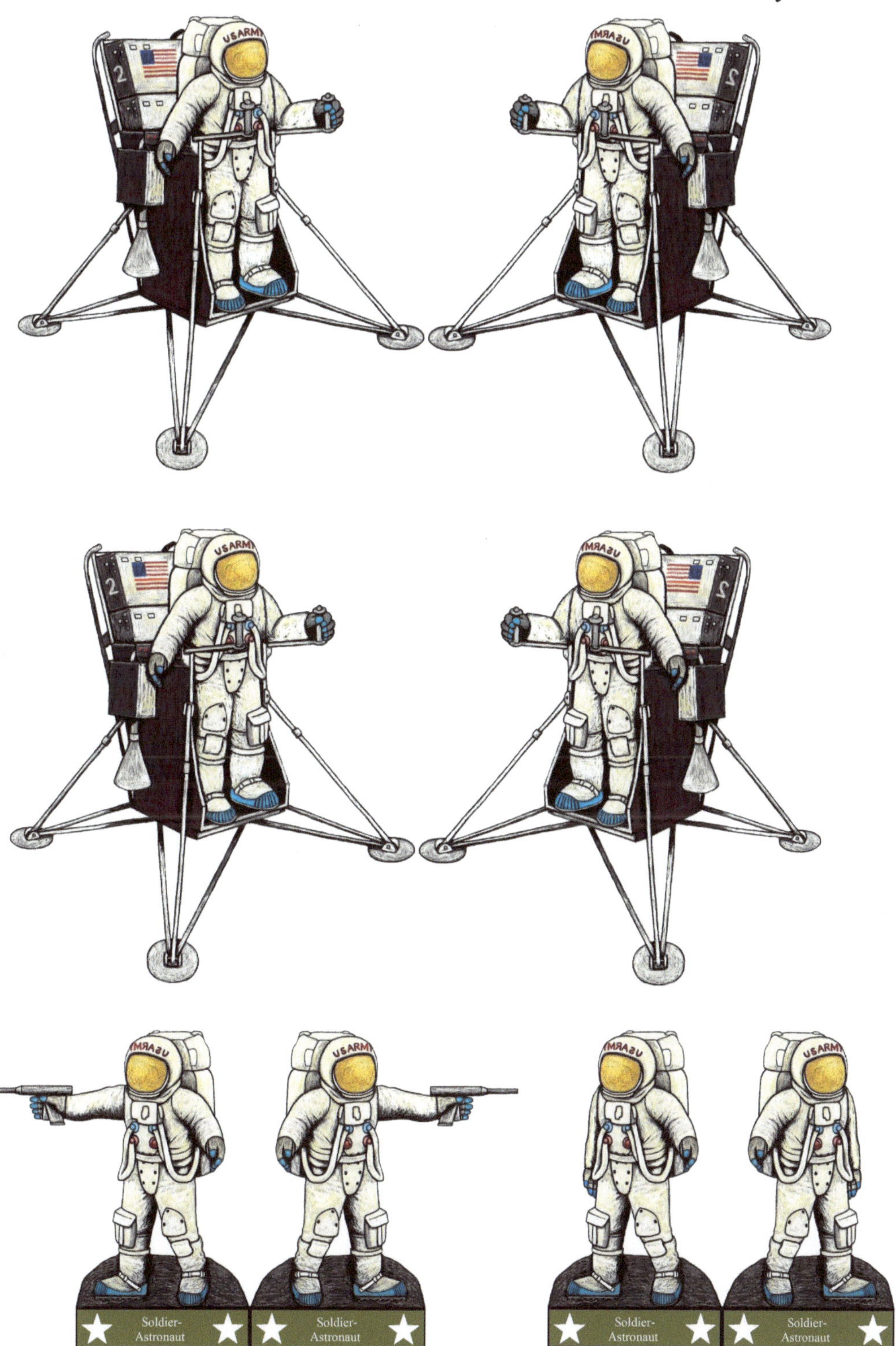

FIGURE PAGE 10 SOLDIER-ASTRONAUT FLYER

If a grid is hit by a meteor. A crater model is placed in the centre, and AREA EFFECT RULES (4.2) are used. The table is divided by the RED LINE: a borderline between each combatant's territory. Each grid square is used for a unit's initial deployment.

If players want they can increase the number of grid squares on their table from six to twelve using two dice to make a determination.

CONQUEST

If a player's unit successfully routs or destroys another unit they are allowed to 'plant the flag' on that location. The more locations clamed allows a player to declare 'Victory' over their opponent, and have extended their nation's Lunar territory.

ANNEX LIST OF 1/72 [1:72, 1:76] HO-SCALE MAKERS OF ASTRONAUTS AND MODEL SPACE CRAFT

The selection of figures and accessories, listed in this Annex are an example list only of the currently available models and figures made by various 1/72 [1:72, 1:76] HO-Scale makers of Astronauts and model Spacecraft. This list is by no means meant to be exhaustive nor are these figures particularly recommended. Merely these are suggested as possible options for use in 1960s Era Lunar Surface wargaming.

AIRFIX 1:76 Astronauts.

B.U.M. (Barcelona Universal Models) No. 0127 1:72 Moon Astronauts.

DRAGON 11002 1/72 Apollo 11 Lunar Landing. CSM Columbia+ LM Eagle + Astronauts Plastic Kit.

DRAGON 11012 1/72 Apollo Soyuz Test Project.

DRAGON 11013 1/72 Gemini Spacecraft.

DRAGON 11015 1/72 Apollo 17 The Last J-Mission. CSM + LM + Lunar Rover Plastic Model Kit.

PEGASUS HOBBY 1/72 Astronaut and Spacecraft Model Kit - HHB022 (Caesar Set HB21 Astronauts and Spacecraft).

SPACE HELMET MODELS 1:72 Apollo XVII Astronauts on the Moon.

LARSON DESIGNS No. 0 1:72 Soviet LK Moon Lander.

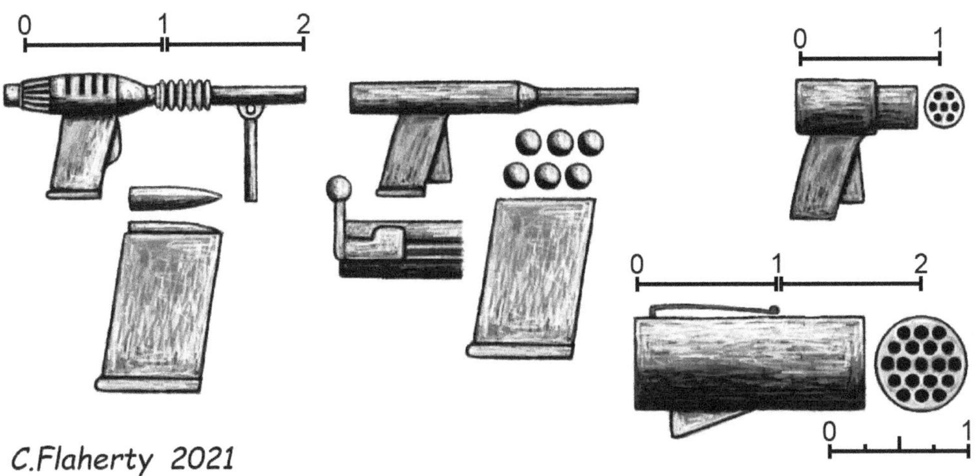

C.Flaherty 2021

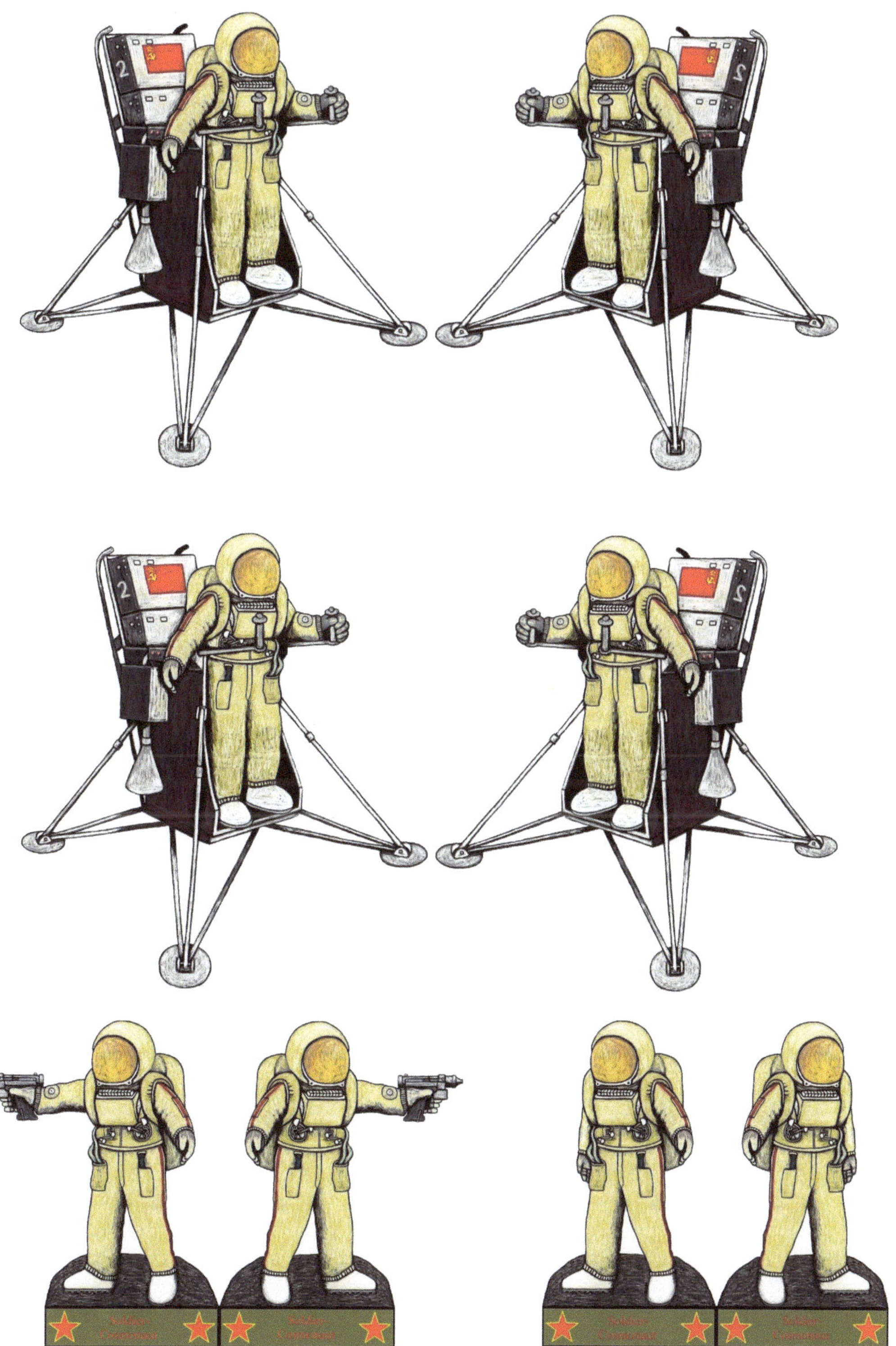

FIGURE PAGE 11 SOLDIER-COSMONAUT FLYER

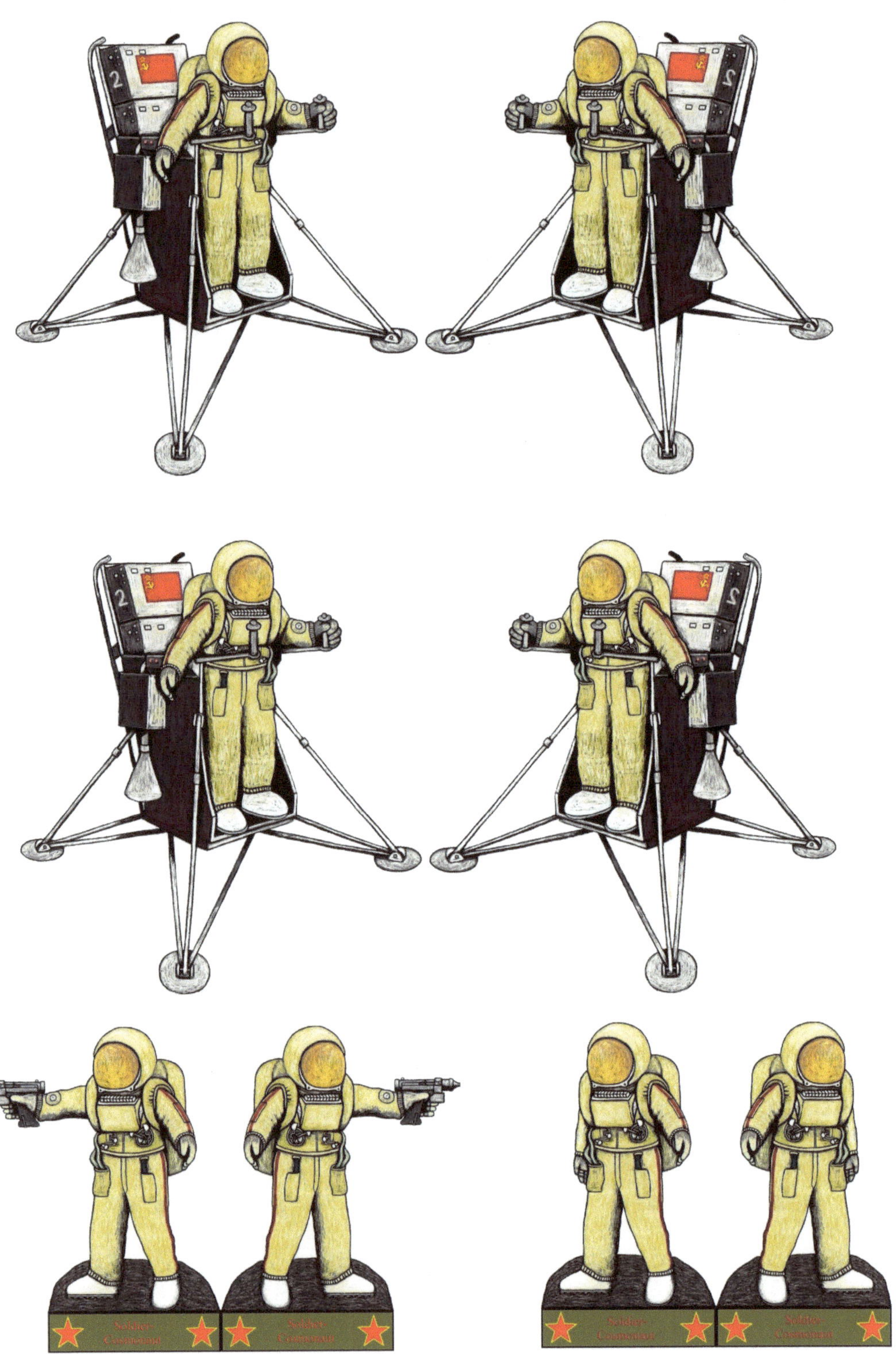

C.Flaherty 2021

FIGURE PAGE 12 SOLDIER-COSMONAUT FLYER

CHAPTER 5: PAPER CUT-OUT ASTRONAUT ARMIES

The book includes templates for miniature Soldier-Astronauts armies to cut out and mount on stands. The pages with figures can be carefully separated from the rest of the book. Once the sheet that you need is separated it is time to assemble your figures. To begin with you will only need two of the pages (we have provided several so you have a lot of spare figures that can be used later if you so wish). For your first game to get used to the rules you will only need three two figure teams of Soldier-Astronauts, and three two figure teams of Soldier-Cosmonauts.

To begin cutting-out the figures, gluing the two sides together, and assembling the completed figure onto a base, you will need the following tools, so you can do a good job:

1. Strong paper glue.

2. Scissors and cutter to cut cardstock.

3. Ruler for straight cuts and an awl tool to cut the lines to be folded.

4. Plastic/Gum mat base to cut and avoid ruining the table.

5. Card to make the base (grey board, corrugated card or kraft card is ideal).

We recommend that only an adult should cut the figures out at all times. The publisher and the authors of the book assume no responsibility for any injuries sustained while making your figures.

Although the figures can be cut out with scissors, the finished effect is likely neater if a sharp knife is used. We recommend an impact adhesive for gluing the pieces together.

The fold connecting the two sides should be partially scored through with your knife, or the point of the scissors, before it is bent-over. If you accidentally cut right through a fold that is not a problem as the two sides can still be glued together.

FIGURE PAGE 1 SOLDIER-ASTRONAUT/COSMONAUT INFANTRY

FIGURE PAGE 2 SOLDIER-ASTRONAUT/COSMONAUT INFANTRY

FIGURE PAGE 3 SOLDIER-ASTRONAUT/COSMONAUT INFANTRY

FIGURE PAGE 4 SOLDIER-ASTRONAUT/COSMONAUT INFANTRY

FIGURE PAGE 5 SOLDIER-ASTRONAUT ROVER TEAM

FIGURE PAGE 6 SOLDIER-ASTRONAUT ROVER TEAM

FIGURE PAGE 7 SOLDIER-COSMONAUT ROVER TEAM

FIGURE PAGE 8 SOLDIER-COSMONAUT ROVER TEAM

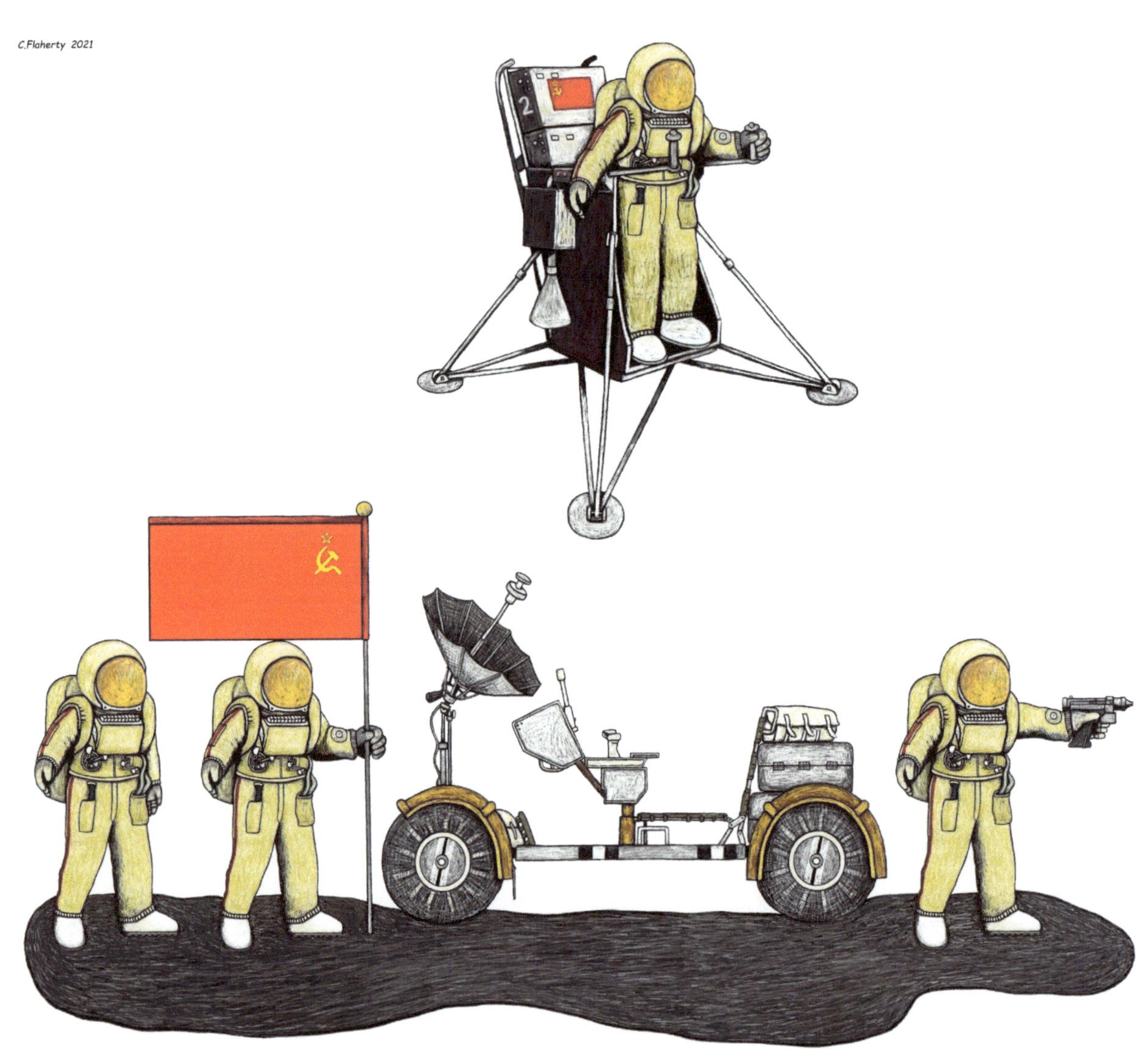
C.Flaherty 2021

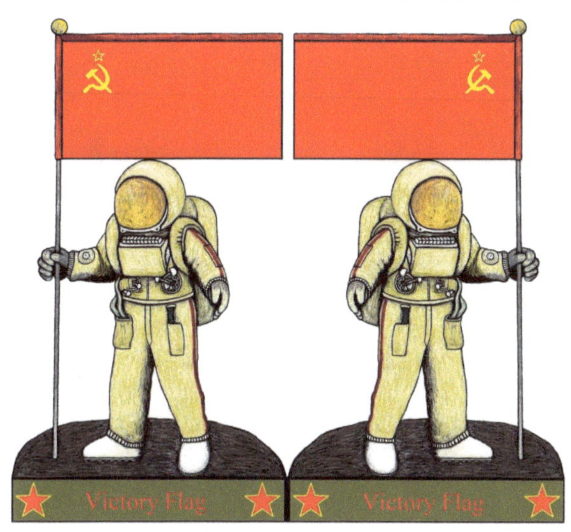

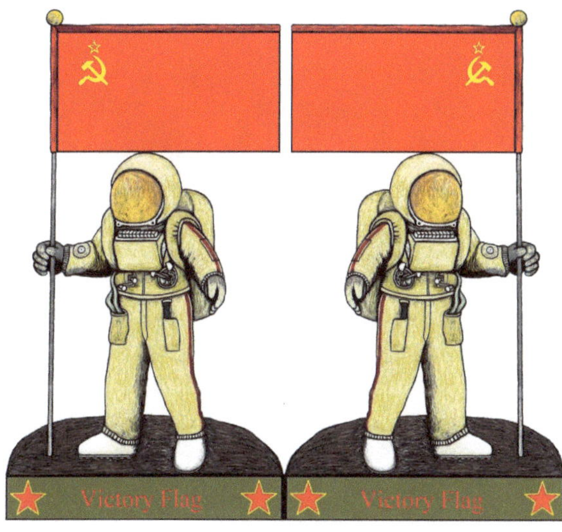

C.Flaherty 2021

FIGURE PAGE 13 VICTORY FLAGS

▲ On the surface of a Moon, near the Red Planet a Cosmonaut is armed with a captured U.S. Gyrojet Projectile Firing Micro Gun.

CHAPTER 6: A LUNAR SURFACE WARGAMING SCENARIO

INTRODUCTION

The main Space Base and Lunar Strategic Missile Strike Force has never been fully operational, and is only capable of launching a limited strike on the Earth's Surface – while potentially devastating, the other powers have been progressively building their own Earth Orbiting Battle Stations that have become an effective strategic counter, and the prospect of MAD: Mutual Assured Destruction has maintained some global stability. On the Moon, two powers have partial control, and constantly probe, and annoy each other along the RED LINE. The immense costs, and logistical complexity of maintaining a presence on the Moon largely restricts both sides.

THE BATTLE BEGINS

In Circumlunar Orbit the Intermediate Orbiting Space Station (and its Space Docks) come over head. At the southwest coast of Mare Imbrium: Sea of Showers, a region with a diameter of 1,123 kilometres (32.8°N15.6°W), just north of the Montes Apenninus Mountains, a region with a diameter of 401 kilometres (19.87°N0.03°W), is where the main United States Lunar Base is located. Some 20 nautical miles north lay a deep-buried Concealed Outpost Base Number 4 of the U.S. Army Taskforce of Soldier-Astronauts. A Lunar Flying Vehicle-Unit takes-off for a patrol from another dummy-base at some distance. The only sign that there is a base at all, is a sloping ramp leading to a large set of airlock doors at its end. A Lunar Roving Vehicle is parked near this. At some distance a meteor strike is seen, and a U.S. Army Soldier-Astronaut takes-off to investigate. During the flight a Soviet Moon Buggy is sighted, with its crew of two Soldier-Cosmonauts, who are spotted close to the RED LINE. The RED LINE separates United States controlled portion of the Moon, from unclaimed areas, where it was known the Soviets had established a foothold – their Zvezda Moon Base-Train had been recently seen on the move from the Space Station, but its whereabouts was unknown as it had dug-in concealing the base location under the regolith. A FLASH ALERT is immediately sent to Lunar Control Dome, and the Circumlunar Orbital Intermediate Orbiting Space Station. A Space Sub-Commander and their three Concealed Outpost Bases are ordered to send forces out to meet the threat. Each Base has a two-team unit of Soldier-Astronauts with Lunar Roving Vehicles, and Lunar Flying Vehicle-Unit.

THE FIRST ENGAGEMENT

The first engagement takes place when two approaching Soviet Moon Buggy stop, and two-teams of Soldier-Cosmonauts at extreme ranges fire their first rounds. The defending U.S. Army Soldier-Astronauts, have established a concealment hide-shelter using their reversible white and black umbrellas. The U.S. Army Soldier-Astronauts return-fire in the direction of the Soviet position. The extreme range, and optical problems that the Astronauts, and Cosmonauts both usually experience, are made more difficult for the defending U.S. Army Soldier-Astronauts as they have only recently arrived from Earth, and apart from training have never been involved in a real Space battle!

THE SOVIET COMMANDER RESPONDS

The Soviet commander unable to work-out where the U.S. Army Soldier-Astronaut Picket might be, or where their Concealed Outpost Bases are located orders a Creeping Barrage Assault. The advancing Soldier-Cosmonauts fire at extreme range their weapons along a front in the hope of suppressing their opponent, either leading to confusion and a withdrawal, or an actual killing, or destruction of equipment – in either way they might be able to push the RED LINE.

REFERENCES

Baker, H. 2021 How Long Would it Take to Walk Around the Moon? Livescience.com (3 April).

Borch, F.L. 2021 Soldiers on the Moon?!? The Army's Strange but True Plan for a Lunar Outpost. The Army Historical Foundation.

Boushey, H.A. 1958 Lunar Base Vital. Army-Navy-Air Force Register. Number 79 (8 February).

Clarke, A.C. 1945 V2 for Ionosphere Research? Wireless World (February).

Clarke, A.C. 1945 [-1968] The Space-Station: Its Radio Applications. Spaceflight. Volume 10. Number 3 (March).

Day, D.A. Kennedy, R.G. 2010 Soviet Star Wars: The Launch that Saved the World from Orbiting Laser Battle Stations. Air & Space Magazine (January).

Dolman, E.C. 2002 Astropolitik: Classical Geopolitics in the Space Age. Frank Cass Publishers.

Gault, M. 2013 When Earth Dreamed of Nuking the Moon. War is Boring (28 November).

Gruntman, M. 2015 Intercept 1961: The Birth of Soviet Missile Defense (Library of Flight). American Institute of Aeronautics and Astronautics Journal.

Hart, B.H.L. 1920 The Essential Principles of War. United Services Magazine (April).

Ley, W. 1948 (1952 Book Form) The Possibilities for an Invasion Base on the Moon. Mechanix Illustrated (April).

Mizokami, R. 2021 Astronauts Really Could Carry M16s on the Moon. Popular Mechanics (31 March).

NASA. Lunar Roving Vehicle.

Portree, D.S.F. 2013 Rocket Belts and Rocket Chairs: Lunar Flying Units (1969). Wired.com (18 July).

Reesman, R. Wilson, J.R. 2020 The Physics of Space War: How Orbital Dynamics Constrain Space-to-Space Engagements. The Aerospace Corporation (October).

Reiffel, L. 1959 A Study of Lunar Research Flights. Air Force Special Weapons Center (19 June).

Remuss, N-L. 2011 Astronauts: From Envoys of Mankind to Combatants. Schrogl, K-U. Landfester, U. Remuss, N-L. Worms, J-C. (Editors) Humans in Outer Space — Interdisciplinary Perspectives. Springer-Verlag Wien.

Sambaluk, N.M. 2011 What's a Heaven For? National Public Culture's Role in Shaping U.S. Space Policy, Aerospace Doctrine, and the Future of the Dyna-Soar, 1957-61. Dissertation. The University of Kansas.

Smith, W.H.B. Pegg, T.M. 1983 Small Arms of the World. New York: Stackpole Books.

Thomas, K.S. Mcentimetersann, H.J. 2006 US Spacesuits. Chichester, UK: Praxis Publishing Ltd.

Trevithick, J. 2021 Here's Our Best Look Yet at Russia's Secretive Space Cannon, the Only Gun Ever Fired in Space. The War Zone (16 February).

United Nations. Office for Outer Space Affairs (UNOOSA). Resolution Adopted by The General Assembly 2222 (XXI). Treaty on Principles Governing the Activities of States in the Exploration and Use of Outer Space, Including the Moon and Other Celestial Bodies.

U.S. Airforce [United States Airforce]. 1961 Lunar Expedition Plan (Lunex). Headquarters Space Systems Division, Air Force Systems Command (May).

U.S. Army [United States Army]. 1965 The Meanderings of a Weapon Oriented Mind When Applied in a Vacuum Such as on the Moon. Headquarters Weapons Command Rock Island, Illinois (June, 652156).

U.S. Army [United States Army]. 1959 Project Horizon Report: A U. S. Army Study for the Establishment of a Lunar Outpost. Volume I: Summary and Supporting Considerations (9 June).

Witt (de), J.K. Edwards, W.B. Scott-Pandorf, M.M. Norcross, J.R. Gernhardt, M.L. 2014 The Preferred Walk to Run Transition Speed in Actual Lunar Gravity. Journal of Experimental Biology. Volume 217. Issue 18.

Zak, A. 2018 The Soviet Laser Space Pistol, Revealed. Popular Mechanics (14 June).

Zak, A. 2016 The Soviet Union's Secret Moon Base That Never Was. Popular Mechanic (11 February).

Zak, A. 2015 Here is the Soviet Union's Secret Space Cannon. Popular Mechanics (16 November).

Zak, A. 2001 [-2021] Origin of the Almaz Project. Russian Space Web.com.

PAPER BATTLE&DIORAMAS PUBLISHED AND IN WORKING

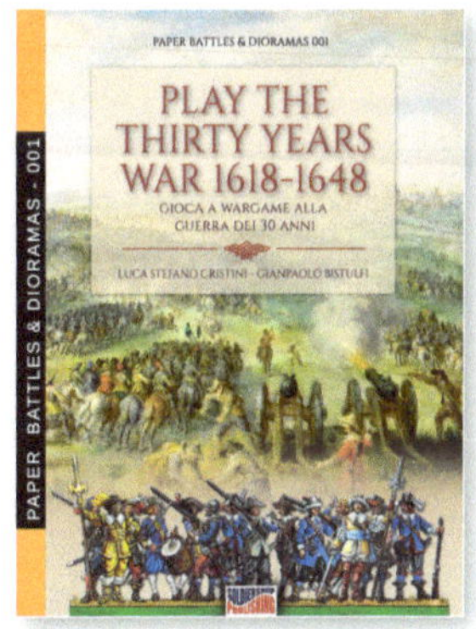

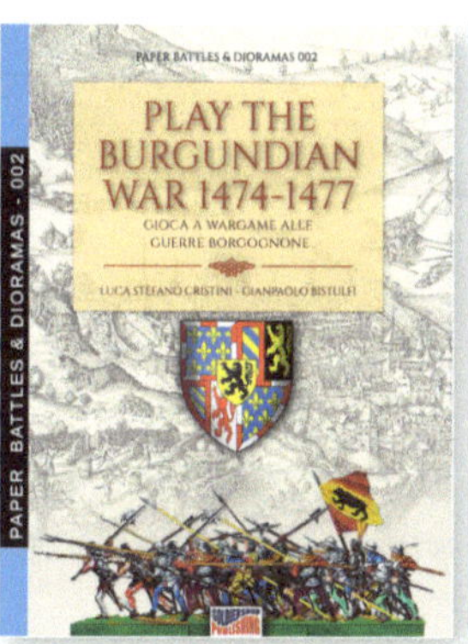

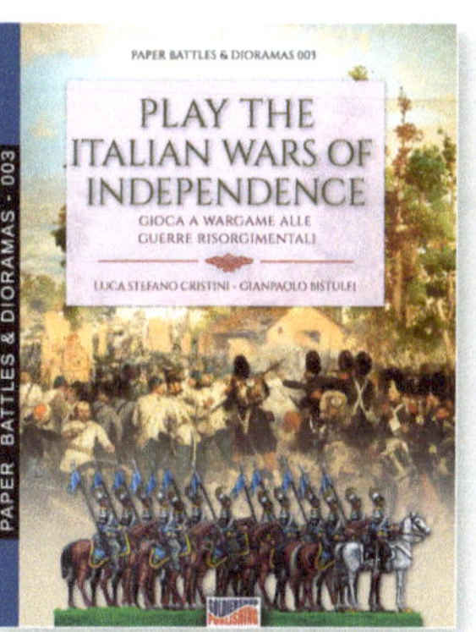

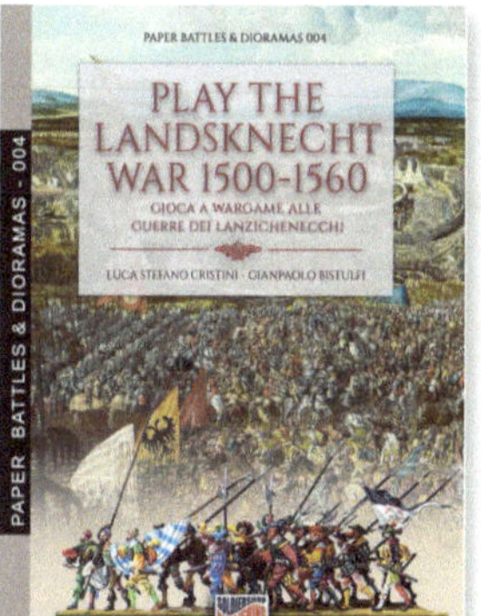

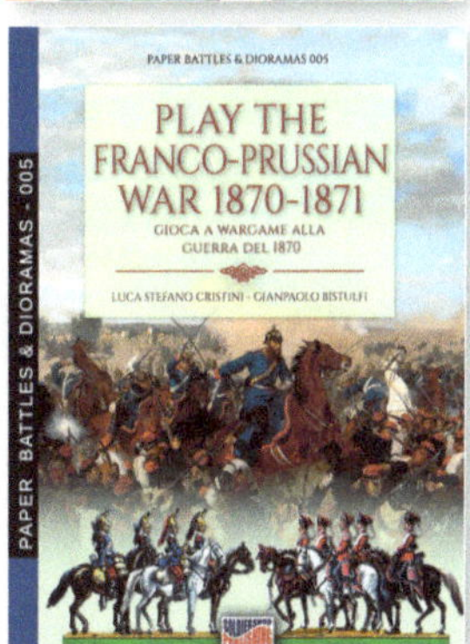

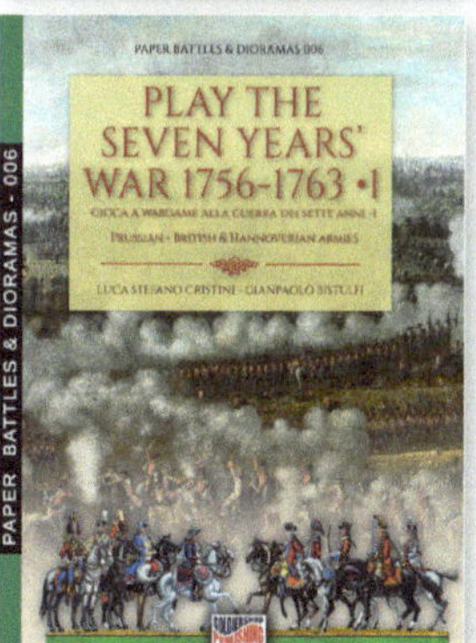

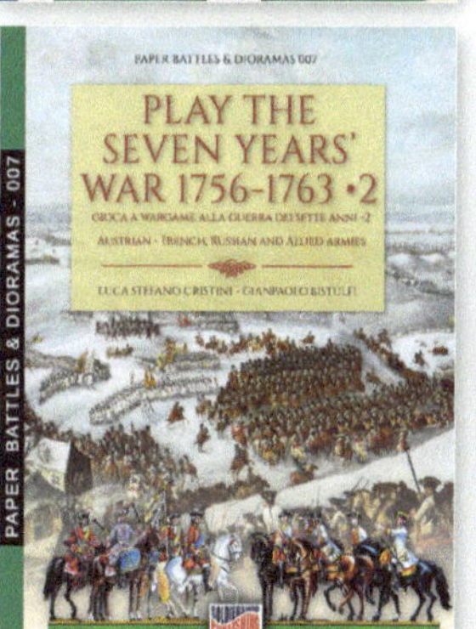

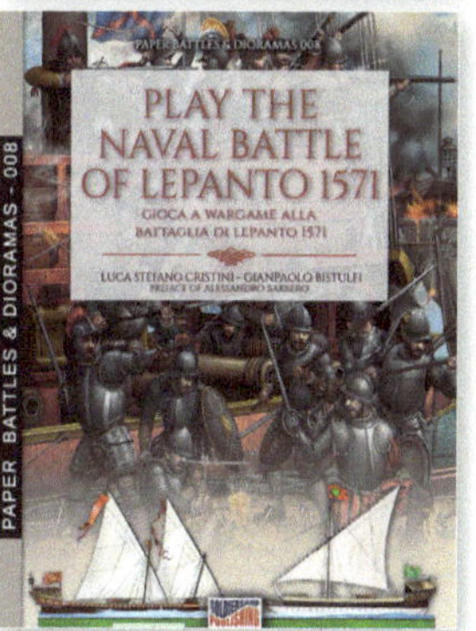

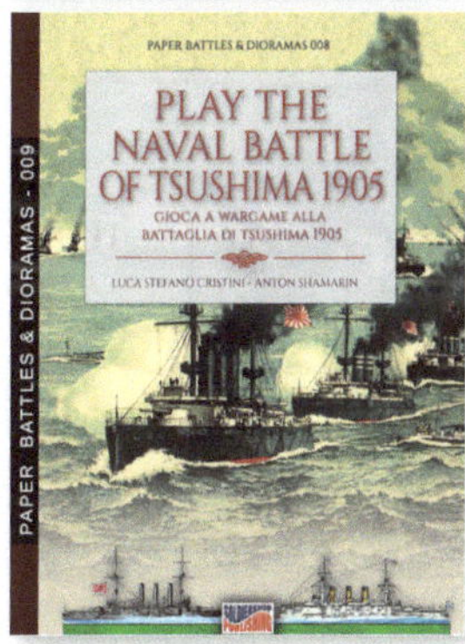

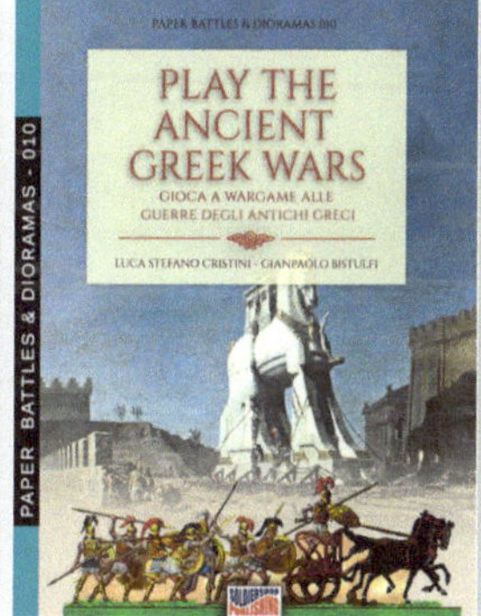

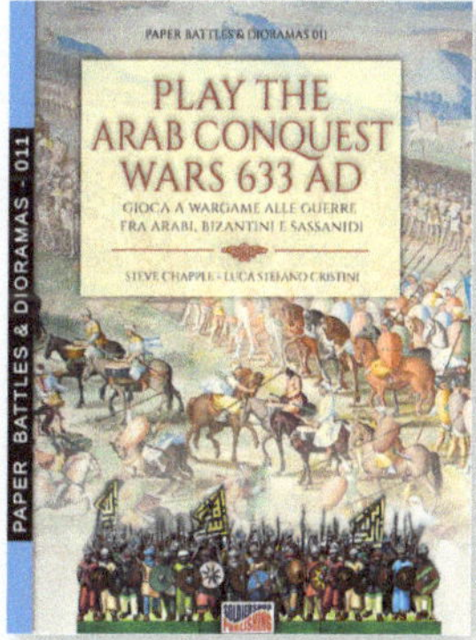

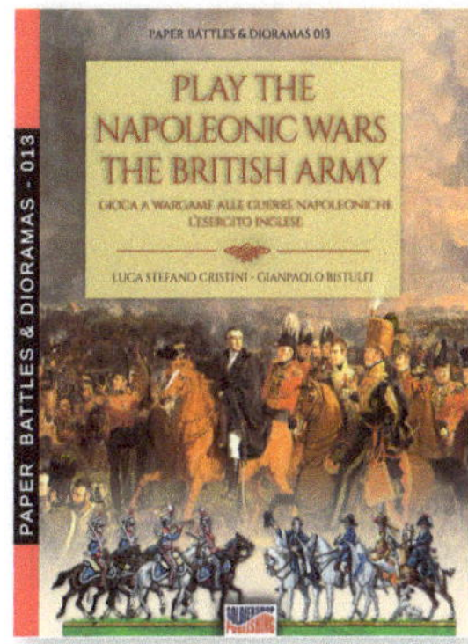

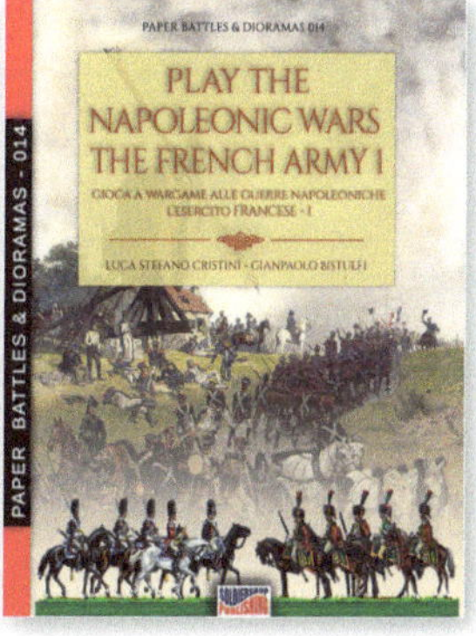

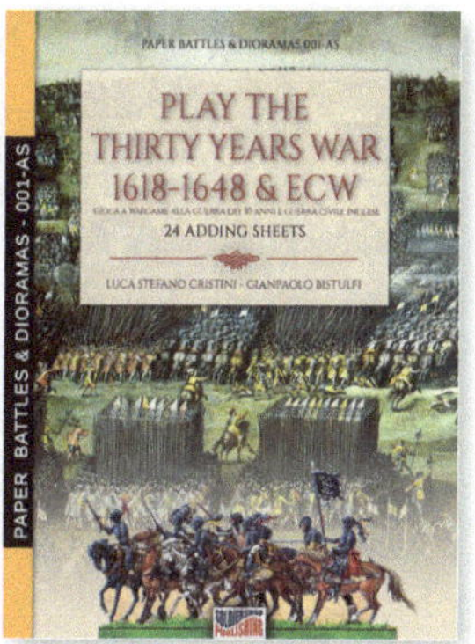

SOLDIERSHOP
PUBLISHING

CRI
STI
NI
ED
ITO
RE

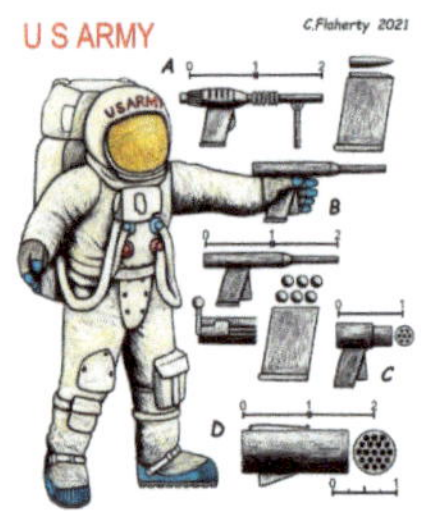

U S ARMY
C.Flaherty 2021
USARM

www.ingramcontent.com/pod-product-compliance
Lightning Source LLC
LaVergne TN
LVHW071610180726
843512LV00003B/611